CASE STUDIES IN

CULTURAL ANTHROPOLOGY

GENERAL EDITORS

George and Louise Spindler

STANFORD UNIVERSITY

THE HUTTERITES IN NORTH AMERICA

THE HUTTERITES
IN NORTH AMERICA

JOHN A. HOSTETLER

and

GERTRUDE ENDERS HUNTINGTON

HARCOURT BRACE COLLEGE PUBLISHERS

Fort Worth   Philadelphia   San Diego   New York   Orlando   Austin   San Antonio
Toronto   Montreal   London   Sydney   Tokyo

Publisher	Ted Buchholz
Editor in Chief	Christopher P. Klein
Senior Acquisitions Editor	Stephen T. Jordan
Assistant Editor	Linda Wiley/Margaret McAndrew Beasley
Project Editor	Tamara Neff Vardy
Production Manager	George H. Smyser
Art Director	Garry Harman

Requests for permission to make copies of any part of the work should be mailed to: Permissions Department, Harcourt Brace & Company, 6277 Sea Harbor Drive, Orlando, Florida 32887-6777.

Address editorial correspondence to:
Harcourt Brace College Publishers
301 Commerce Street, Suite 3700
Fort Worth, TX 76102

Address orders to:
Harcourt Brace & Company
6277 Sea Harbor Drive
Orlando, FL 32887-6777
1-800-782-4479 outside Florida
1-800-433-0001 inside Florida

PRINTED IN THE UNITED STATES OF AMERICA

ISBN: 0-15-502915-0

Library of Congress Catalog Card Number: 95-076783

5 6 7 8 9 0 1 2 3 4 066 9 8 7 6 5 4 3 2 1

Foreword

ABOUT THE SERIES

These case studies in cultural anthropology are designed for students in beginning and intermediate courses in the social sciences, to bring them insights into the richness and complexity of human life as it is lived in different ways, in different places. The authors are men and women who have lived in the societies they write about and who are professionally trained as observers and interpreters of human behavior. Also, the authors are teachers; in their writing, the needs of the student reader remain foremost. It is our belief that when an understanding of ways of life very different from one's own is gained, abstractions and generalizations about the human condition become meaningful.

The scope and character of the series has changed constantly since we published the first case studies in 1960, in keeping with our intention to represent anthropology as it is. We are concerned with the ways in which human groups and communities are coping with the massive changes wrought in their physical and sociopolitical environments in recent decades. We are also concerned with the ways in which established cultures have solved life's problems. And we want to include representation of the various modes of communication and emphasis that are being formed and re-formed as anthropology itself changes.

We think of this series as an instructional series, intended for use in the classroom. We, the editors, have always used case studies in our teaching, whether for beginning students or advanced graduate students. We start with case studies, whether from our own series or from elsewhere, and weave our way into theory, and then turn again to cases. For us, they are the grounding of our discipline.

ABOUT THE AUTHORS

John A. Hostetler, born of Amish parentage in Pennsylvania, is Emeritus Professor of Anthropology and Sociology at Temple University. He holds a Ph.D. from The Pennsylvania State University. He has done fieldwork in rural communities in the United States and Canada, and in Switzerland and southern Germany as a Fulbright Scholar, and has taught at the University of Alberta. He has written several books including *Amish Society* (1993) and professional articles dealing with social anthropology and problems of marginal persons. John Hostetler is internationally known for his research on the Amish and Mennonite communities in the United States and for his work among the Hutterites in this country and in Canada. He has served as an expert witness in a number of legal cases involving education and environmental problems of minority cultures, and has served as a consultant for the Smithsonian

Institution, the National Geographic Society, the National Film Board of Canada, and National Public Radio.

Gertrude Enders Huntington, an anthropologist, teaches at The University of Michigan in Ann Arbor, Michigan. She attended Oberlin College and was graduated from Swarthmore College, attended Rochester University, and holds a Ph.D. degree from Yale University. She has taught biology, done fieldwork in Turkey, and wrote a five-volume dissertation entitled "Dove at the Window: A Study of an Old Order Amish Community in Ohio" and published professionally on the Amish and Hutterites. She served as principal fieldworker on the Hutterite Socialization Study, of which John A. Hostetler was project director. She, her mother, husband, and three children lived in a Hutterite colony for an extended period.

ABOUT THIS CASE STUDY

The authors describe in intimate detail the day-to-day living patterns of the Hutterites, a communal group living in the Great Plains of the United States and Canada. This personalistic treatment of the materials allows the reader to empathize fully with the Hutterites as persons.

As a group, Hutterites are protected from the outside world by a well-organized belief system, which offers a solution to their every need. The Hutterite community minimizes aggression and dissension of any kind. Members strive to lose their self-identity by surrendering themselves to the "communal will," and attempt to live each day in preparation for death, and hopefully heaven. It is not surprising, therefore, that the Hutterites have retained their solidarity despite the persecution of surrounding neighbors.

The authors—careful students of Amish society, a society resembling the Hutterites in many aspects—view the principle of order as a key concept underlying the Hutterite way of life. Order is synonymous with eternity and godliness; even the orientation of colony buildings conforms to directions measured with the precision of a compass. There is a proper order for every activity, and time is neatly divided into the sacred and the secular. In the divine hierarchy of the community, each individual member has a place—male over female, husband over wife, older over younger, and parent over child. It is also noteworthy that the Hutterites find the rigidity of German syntax (which is applied whenever possible) supportive of their hierarchical systematizing.

The meaning of persecution is brought vividly to the fore by the description of the inhumane treatment of four young Hutterite men who refused military service in World War I because of their religious convictions. We think of torture and deprivation to force submission to duly constituted authority as something done in other countries. That it happened in the "land of the free" is a measure of the potentially deadly prejudice against difference that lurks in the shadows of duly constituted authority, even in a free society. The Hutterites have lived with prejudice since their beginnings four and one-half centuries ago. Every school child is taught about their history of persecution at the hands of state and church authority, and it is never far from consciousness throughout life.

The Hutterites are interesting in their own right but also because they are a challenge to the central values nourishing North American mainstream culture. Nonaggression, selflessness, and humility are core social and personal values for Hutterites, in opposition to achievement, exploitation, and aggression patterned deeply into mainstream culture. George Spindler was once told by a Hutterite youth, "George, you couldn't stand to be Hutterite for three seconds!" He was right. The oppositions run too deep. Above all, the loss of personal freedom in a strictly communal society with a rigid *ordnung* would be unbearable for most mainstream Americans. We can admire the Hutterites for sticking to their "difference" so doggedly.

The Hutterites are a shining example how education maintains community. The proper raising of the young is *a,* if not *the,* primary concern of all Hutterite colonies, and despite laws in the United States and Canada that define how much schooling shall be required and of what the curriculum should consist, the Hutterites manage to teach their children the Hutterite way of life, even the language, with school time and institutions of their own. And the colony itself is a school. Children grow up surrounded and monitored by adults who look much alike and think and believe much alike. Hutterite education is highly successful, if success is measured by how well education transmits culture and maintains community.

A closed community such as that of the Hutterites is a difficult setting for ethnographic work. The anthropologist must be accepted into the inner circle of life to understand how a culture works. John Hostetler, raised as an Amishman, had an affinity for Hutterite culture, and Gertrude Huntington acquired one. The story of their fieldwork among the Hutterites is printed in Appendix A of this case study. For some readers, it should be the first thing they read.

As teachers of introductory cultural anthropology at Stanford, we have often used this case study in conjunction with the films listed at the end of this volume. The combination of film and case study makes an unbeatable instructional unit that illustrates significant aspects of communal life and of an important minority group in North American society.

George and Louise Spindler
Ethnographics
P.O. Box 38, Calistoga, CA, 94515

Contents

CASE STUDIES IN

CULTURAL ANTHROPOLOGY

GENERAL EDITORS

George and Louise Spindler

STANFORD UNIVERSITY

THE HUTTERITES IN NORTH AMERICA

Introduction

Hutterites are attempting to establish a colony of heaven. They do not have illusory ideas that their colony is perfect, but they have acquired some utopian-like characteristics in their social patterns such as economy of human effort, elimination of extremely poor or wealthy members, a system of distribution that minimizes privileged position, motivation without the incentive of private gain, and a high degree of security for the individual. All of these characteristics are contained in a communal society without the use of a police force and with an ideology that reasonably satisfies both their spiritual and material needs.

By living on large acreages of communally owned land, the Hutterites maintain a degree of geographic isolation. Their German dialect and distinctive dress reinforce social isolation from their neighbors. The Hutterites think of themselves as a people who honor God properly by living communally. Honoring God, they say, requires communal living, devout pacifism, and proper observance of religious practices. They regard as inevitable the atrocities they have suffered throughout their history, as well as the misunderstandings with the outside world in modern times. To the Hutterites, suffering is a necessity for which they must be morally prepared at all times. During four-and-one-half centuries, the group has demonstrated a remarkable ability to adapt to changing political, social, and technological environments. The Hutterites are the largest family-type communal group in the Western world. The society is noted for successful large-scale farming, large families, and effective training of the young. These distinguishing features are inseparable from their religion. All Hutterites inhabit the United States and Canada and none have survived in the countries of their origin, namely Austrian Tyrol and Moravia. In 1994 the population numbered about 35,000 persons in 382 colonies.

The Hutterites originated during the Protestant Reformation in the sixteenth century and are one of three surviving Anabaptist groups. The other two are the Mennonites (Smith 1981) and the Swiss Anabaptists including the Old Order Amish (Hostetler 1993). The Anabaptists were nonconformist groups who rejected infant baptism and membership in a state or all-inclusive church. Instead of reforming the medieval church, the Anabaptists wanted to withdraw from its influences entirely and establish voluntary church groups. Their views challenged existing social, economic, and political institutions as well as those of the great reformers including Martin Luther. Many became martyrs. With the collapse of feudalism of the Middle Ages, there were many landless persons—artisans and craftsmen along with scholars —who joined newly formed movements such as the Anabaptists. They were the less privileged of their day, and the nonconformist movements offered a new psychological outlook on life. Equipped with the justification for denying earlier traditions, they substituted small voluntary groups for the traditional social hierarchy of feudal society. Various Anabaptists wished to establish a Christian-type community in which private property would be abolished and temporal possessions would be surrendered voluntarily by the individual (Klaassen 1964). Of many attempts at forming "communities of love" only the Hutterites successfully and permanently carried out communal living. In their early period Hutterites were a "conversionist" type of sect, but in their more recent history they approximate the "introversionist" type (Wilson 1959), avoiding involvement with the larger society.

The Hutterites regard 1528 as their founding date (Hutterian Brethren, 1987:80–82). While fleeing from Nikolsburg to Austerlitz, a group of religious refugees introduced the practice of "community of goods." Each person heaped all of his possessions on cloaks that had been spread on the ground, and stewards were selected as overseers of the material goods. Thus, occasioned by necessity and sanctioned by religion, communal sharing was made the norm. The first common household (*Bruderhof* or colony) was founded in Austerlitz in Moravia. Jacob Hutter of Tyrol joined the community and greatly intensified the discipline. He was captured by the authorities, interrogated, brutally whipped, and burned at the stake in 1536. Although not the founder of the Hutterites, who are named after him, Hutter was their most outstanding organizer and leader.

The Hutterites were tolerated for a time by local barons of Moravia who found them to be outstanding farmers and craftsmen. During this time of tolerance and protection they experienced growth and prosperity. They expanded to approximately eighty colonies with an estimated population of about 20,000 persons (Rideman 1950:275). Their colonies were large and well-managed. Their activities in addition to agriculture included ceramics, cutlery, milling, wine making, spinning, weaving, tailoring, clock making, and carriage making. Their mineral baths achieved a wide reputation. Hutterite nurses, midwives, and physicians were in great demand. All young men learned a trade. The schools were systematic, compulsory for children of members, and were attended by non-Hutterites. Virtually all of the members were literate.

Prosperity was followed by growing intolerance. The enemies of the Hutterites were not only religious and political, but soon there developed economic envy and antagonisms. They were accused of monopoly. The Hutterite workers were thrifty, motivated, and efficient, and myths of Hutterite wealth spread widely, which later induced raids and robbery. Their pacifistic communism, disinterest in politics, and refusal to fight on any side in a war rendered their future precarious.

With the outbreak of war between Austria and Turkey in 1593 the Hutterites were raided by both Austrian and Turkish armies. At first they were heavily taxed, then robbed, plundered, tortured, and many were executed or sent into captivity. The disastrous Thirty Years' War followed, and by 1622 all the Hutterites had been driven from Moravia. Slovakia and several small states to the east, including Transylvania and Wallachia, became host to the group. In Slovakia they rebuilt their communities only to suffer decline, steady pressures from the Jesuits to return to the Catholic faith, and imprisonment. With the elders in prison or in monasteries and the children in orphanages, many accepted Catholicism. A remnant crossed the Carpathian mountains into Wallachia in 1767 where they were soon caught in the Russo-Turkish War. On invitation from a Russian general, 123 Hutterites settled in Ukraine in 1770.

Although the Hutterites were granted complete religious freedom, exemption from military duty, vast agricultural lands, and free practice of their trades, their privileges were never secure in Russia. Upon achieving reasonable material recovery after so many years of hardship, their best craftsmen exerted their individuality and refused to turn over their profits to the common treasury. Communal ownership was abandoned for forty years, from 1819 to 1859. A period of internal decline, resulting in poverty and illiteracy, was followed by renewal. An extensive religious revival occurred in 1856–1859. Scarcely had the group reinstituted communal living when the Russian government changed its attitude toward German colonists. Expert farmers and settlers were no longer needed. With large numbers of unassimilated Germans living on choice lands in Ukraine, a new nationalization policy was enacted that forced the Hutterites along with many Mennonites, Doukhobours, and other minorities to migrate to North America. The universal military training act of 1872, repealing earlier exemptions, including those granted by Catherine the Great, precipitated their decision to leave the continent.

All Hutterites, numbering nearly 1,200 persons, relocated in South Dakota. Their need for large, isolated blocks of land rendered them ineligible for homesteading privileges. About two-thirds of the families decided to take advantage of homesteading by settling on family farms. These *Prairie-Leut* (prairie people or "noncolony" people), as they were called by the Hutterites, later affiliated with nearby Mennonite groups. The Hutterites founded three colonies in South Dakota between 1874 and 1877, each immigrating at slightly different times. Hutterites today acknowledge three distinct "people" (*Leut*) among them. Taking their names from their first leaders in the United States, they are *Schmied-Leut, Darius-Leut, and*

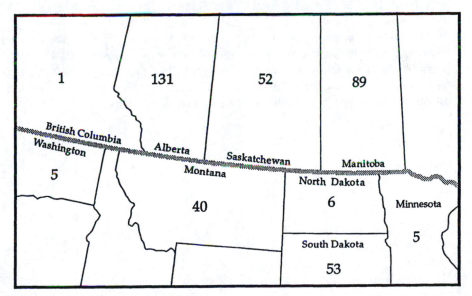

Number of Hutterite colonies in North America

Lehrer-Leut. The three share a common body of doctrine, language and social patterns, but each has its own senior elder and *Ordnung* (discipline). Each *Leut* has its own periodic preacher assembly that ordains leaders and modifies or changes the discipline, and each is unified by the preferred endogamous marriage pattern. The *Leut* is the largest unit within which there is both a means and a moral obligation to settle disputes. The Society of Brothers' (a twentieth-century religious group) attempts to affiliate with the three *Leut* have led to problems and dissension.

The research on which this case study is based was part of a study of communal education in Hutterite society over a period of several years. The units of observation consisted of one colony from each of the three *Leut* and are anonymously referred to in the case study as *Dariushof, Lehrerhof,* and *Schmiedehof,* though they are not necessarily representative of other colonies within the *Leut.* The three colonies observed include respectively a newly formed small colony, an average-sized colony, and a large colony that has had one branching. One is located in the United States and two are in Canada. The three are no closer than 500 miles from each other. The criteria for selecting the three colonies took into account size, age, social and economic practices, and *Leut* affiliation. At the time of the original study, the populations of the three colonies were 55, 101, and 124, respectively, or a combined population of 280 persons in thirty-eight nuclear families. The three colonies in the original study have each branched, forming seven colonies. One colony became closely affiliated with the Society of Brothers. The objective was to observe a small number of people intensively in order to gain a detailed record of interpersonal relations in each of the sample colonies. The data were obtained by direct observation and from conversation while participating in the culture. Information schedules or questionnaires were not used.

In the ensuing years we have maintained contact and have repeatedly visited with members of the sample colonies, in addition to visiting more than 130 additional colonies.

Throughout the case study English equivalents will be given for the German terms peculiar to the culture except when special emphasis is desired. Of the several possible names for the group, such as Hutterian Brethren, *Huterische Brüder or Huterischen,* it was decided to use the more familiar term Hutterites. It is the name established by usage by the group members as well as by others.

1 / World View

Dawn breaks on the vast fields of the prairie, lighting a cluster of buildings hidden in the quiet recesses of a coulee. On a summer morning the colony bell wakes everyone at 6:15 A.M. "Like everyone else," says a Hutterite girl, "I roll out of bed and get dressed, then go down on my knees to thank the good Lord for protection and to get a blessing for the day."

The bell calls the adults to the communal kitchen for a breakfast of prunes, cheese, smoked ham, bread, jam, and coffee. Quickly and in order the men file in, hang their hats on a rack extended from the ceiling, and take their assigned places on benches around a long table. All are dressed in black work trousers and colored shirts, and all of the mature men are bearded. Uniformly garbed women with identical hair styles enter next, wearing polka-dotted head scarfs, long, patterned aprons and dresses. They sit at a second long table separate from the men. The last are scarcely seated when a man gives the audible signal to pray. Instantly everyone raises folded hands and a man mutters a short prayer.

The tabletops shine with new varnish. Each person uses a shallow dish for his individual plate. The bread, on wooden centerpieces, is within reach of each set of four persons. Coffee is poured into cups by the oldest person, who is always seated at the end of the table, and is then passed to each person. No children or babies are present; they have been left in the apartments and will eat separately. The highest officials of the colony, the preacher and his assistant, eat in the preacher's apartment, where food has been brought to them from the central kitchen.

Silence prevails during mealtime. Everyone eats quickly, and breakfast is dismissed with another prayer. Each person carries his own dishes to the kitchen. Women quickly finish clearing the tables and begin washing the dishes. In seven minutes the job is completed.

The bell rings again, this time signaling the children from ages six to fourteen to their dining room. Those from two-and-one-half to five years go to the kindergarten for their breakfast and will remain there for most of the day. The men gather in the shop, where every day begins with each person receiving an assigned responsibility.

Anthropologists who thoroughly familiarize themselves with a culture can formulate the underlying principles that govern behavior patterns. They assume that the patterns of a culture are not random and haphazard but represent a selection based on deep-lying assumptions. All peoples have norms of belief and norms of practice. The beliefs that a people express about the nature of the external world, about man himself, and about the nature of existence have been called existential postulates (Hoebel 1966:23). While these ideals influence the behavior of a society, they are never wholly effective in solving the problems of day-to-day living. Another set of assumptions, called normative postulates, specify whether behavior is good or bad, proper or improper. The existential and normative postulates (also called ideal versus real, or formal versus informal culture patterns) provide individuals in a society with a distinctive orientation toward the world around them and toward each other. This distinctive approach to life, which colors the entire view of things, is known as *Weltanschauung,* or world view. Thus, the rules of living seem natural and right to individuals who have absorbed the world view of their culture. To outsiders who are not of that society they seem strange and unnatural.

The Hutterites draw their ideals from the Christian Bible, the Old and New Testaments, and from the Apocrypha, but their solutions to day-to-day living differ so sharply from most Christian groups that they scarcely bear resemblance to them. The official statement of their faith was written in prison in 1540 by one of their leaders, Peter Rideman (1950). It embodies the Hutterite view of life and death, relation of man to man, and the basis for communal living. Formulated in this chapter are the existential postulates of the Hutterites, based on the Rideman book and on observations in contemporary colonies.

VIEW OF THE UNIVERSE, NATURE, AND SUPERNATURE

Absolute authority emanates from a single supernatural being, an omnipotent God, who created the universe and placed everything in order and harmony. No man can cause events to happen, and all events that affect a person's life are determined by God. Man was made to worship God, the Creator, and not to worship the creation or things made by God. Orientation is toward life after death (eternity) and not toward the enjoyment of the present life, nor toward self-development of the individual.

In their morning and evening prayers, children acknowledge an "eternal God who has wonderfully created all things in Heaven and on earth." In catechism at school they learn the difference between a "right faith" and a "false hope." A right faith is both "living" and "a gift from God," made possible by "believing in God's word," and demonstrated by "pious living" and suffering. When baptized at the age of about twenty, the young adults "establish a covenant with God and all his people" to "give self, soul, and body, with all possessions to the Lord in Heaven." In marriage a spouse is acknowledged as "a gift from God."

Hutterites consider themselves responsible for the maintenance of their own offspring through vigilant daily teaching. "Through attentive hearing and observing of the gospel we become partakers of the community of Christ" (Rideman 1950:43). Maintenance implies not only nurture but vigorous separation from the world. Diligent nurture is required at all times for all ages, from the youngest to the oldest, since "no man is free from the tendency to serve his natural inclinations."

Respect for order and authority pervades Hutterite thought and practice. The natural, including human nature, must obey the supernatural order. The right order regulates all things, the moon and stars, the plants and animals, and also man. Just as day is separated from the night, so God established order among human beings. The right or divine order requires a hierarchy of relationships. One part is always

Colony preacher. He must be conservative in religious values and progressive in work and economic affairs.

superior to the other. The higher cares for, directs, and uses the lower; the lower serves
and obeys the higher. God is Lord over man, man is over woman, and the elder over
the younger. Man has power over the animals. Man is ruler over material things, inventions and machines, and he may use them as long as the proper relationship and
function are observed. Man may not change the order of God. He may not, for example, kill other men, nor may he interfere with the process of natural conception.

The reason for the creation and continuation of the universe, according to the
Hutterites, is that man might honor God. Only those who "submit and surrender" to
God are His children (Rideman 1950:68), and submission is evidenced by forsaking
everything, including property, in order to live communally. God desires to be honored only in His Church and by none other, and the Hutterites believe they are
unique in using "created things" to lead human beings to God on such a narrow path.
Their way of life justifies the existence of man and of the material world that was
created for man's use.

Although sixteenth-century Hutterites were very aggressive in missionary activity (Littell 1958:126), contemporary Hutterites acknowledge their inability to send

out missionaries but apply the missionary directive to vigorous teaching of the young. "Weeding the garden at home," is believed by some colonies to be the first responsibility and, by others, their sole responsibility. Hutterites do not consider themselves responsible for organized missionary work, but when a believing individual approaches the colony, efforts are taken to show the penitent one the correct way.

VIEW OF HUMAN NATURE AND THE OUTSIDE WORLD

Human nature is regarded as evil, fallen, and displeasing to God. Man was made in the image of God, but through the disobedience of the woman and the acquiescence of the man (Rideman 1950:55) in the Garden of Eden, Adam and Eve and their offspring became perverse. Human beings fell from a spiritual nature to a carnal nature, and children are born in sin and with a tendency to desire the carnal.

The individual can be restored to the spiritual nature by believing in the Word of God as interpreted by Hutterite sermons, by repentance of sin (culturally defined misbehavior), and by continuous and daily surrender of self to the will of God in communal living. By thus "dying" to his carnal nature, man can be "born of Christ" and receive a spiritual nature, a nature that will live eternally.

Before the individual is old enough to acknowledge voluntarily his own sinful nature, he is taught to obey God and revere Him as the "Almighty Father." Children are not permitted to carry out their own headstrong and carnal practice, and from the beginning are taught "the divine discipline" (Rideman 1950:130). "Just as iron tends to rust, and soil nourishes weeds if not cultivated, so children require continuous care to keep them from their natural inclinations toward injustices, desires, and lusts," says a seventeenth-century elder, Andreas Ehrenpreis. Baptism is postponed until the threshold of adulthood when full implications of the denial of private property and the acceptance of suffering are understood.

Hutterites view the world dualistically. The carnal nature is temporal and passing and brings spiritual death. By contrast, all who are "born of Christ" are ruled by the spiritual nature, which is eternal. (See Eliade 1961:197, for the recurring theme of the second birth in other religions.) The two kingdoms are separate and each must go its separate way. It follows that Hutterites aim to live separate from the (carnal) world with their loyalties rooted in the spiritual. Separation is ordained by God, says Rideman (1950:112, 139, 140, 187). "Many tribes call themselves Christian but they do not wish for the Kingdom of God and Christ. The Kingdom of God is the cross, tribulation, suffering, and persecution, to drink the bitter wine of suffering and to help Him carry His cross. They [other professing Christians] neglect such suffering. They do not like to be hated by the world" (Rideman 1950:3).

The separation between the carnal and the spiritual world is maintained on the informal level. Hutterite loyalty has been tested by scorn, persecution, and martyrdom throughout their history. The many accounts of persecution in their chronicles are transmitted to each new generation to impress upon the young the price of absolute loyalty to communal living.

Two accounts, one from the sixteenth century and one from the twentieth century, illustrate the cost of faithfulness. The Hutterite *Chronicle* (Hutterian Brethren,

1987:343–344) gives this account of an Anabaptist taken prisoner: "Hans Král was taken prisoner for his witness to Jesus Christ and the divine truth. He was traveling for God's cause when he was captured. . . . They put him in a deep, pitch-dark dungeon in the castle. . . . His clothes rotted away on his body until he was almost naked, and for a long time he had no shirt. . . . There he lay in the terrible dungeon that was so full of worms and vermin. . . . The rats and mice even ate his food. When the meals were let down to him . . . he had to be sure to get hold of the bowl before it reached the ground. Otherwise the vermin would be all over it before he had a chance."

Král nearly perished in the dungeon. Many of his contemporaries died and others lost their limbs as a result of imprisonment in the stocks. On the way to the gallows Král escaped and returned to become a leader of the Hutterite colonies in Moravia.

He composed a song about his experiences in prison, a song that is still sung today in Hutterite colonies (Hütterischen Brüder 1962:538).

Hutterite school children today will draw pictures of the martyrs, the rivers in which they were drowned , the castles where they served time in prison, and the fires which burned them to death.

A second illustration of Hutterite loyalty occurred in the United States. In 1918 a group of young Hutterite men in South Dakota were summoned for army duty (Hostetler 1974:129). They obeyed orders to appear at Camp Lewis, but there they refused to sign induction papers, to put on army uniforms, or to take up any kind of duty, on grounds that they were religious objectors to war. After two months in the guard house, four young Hutterite men were sentenced to thirty-seven years in prison. They were taken to the notorious military prison on the island of Alcatraz in San Francisco Bay. Four armed lieutenants attended the young pacifists, who were handcuffed during the day and chained by the ankles to each other by night. At Alcatraz they were ordered to remove their outer clothing and put on military uniforms, but they refused. They were taken to the "dungeon" of darkness, filth, and stench where they were placed in solitary confinement. The guard placed a uniform in each cell and said, "There you will stay until you give up the ghost—just like the last four that we carried out yesterday."

For several days the young men slept on the cold, wet concrete floor wearing nothing but their light underwear. They received a half glass of water every twenty-four hours but no food. They were placed at distances that made it impossible for them to speak to one another. They were beaten with clubs and, with arms crossed, were tied to the ceiling. After five days they were taken from the "hole" for a short time. Their wrists were so swollen from insect bites and skin eruptions that they could not put on their own jackets. For the remaining months at Alcatraz they were allowed one hour of outdoor exercise each Sunday afternoon.

After four months at Alcatraz, the men were transferred to Fort Leavenworth, Kansas, by six armed sergeants. They arrived at their destination at 11 P.M., after four days and five nights of travel, chained together two by two. From the railway station to the military prison they were driven on foot through the streets and prodded with bayonets. Although they were handcuffed they managed to carry their satchels in one hand and their Bibles in the other. On arrival at the prison, soaked with sweat, they were compelled to remove their outer clothing. Two hours later, when they received their prison clothing, they were chilled to the bone. In the early morning hours they stood outside and waited in the cold. Joseph and Michael Hofer collapsed and were taken to the hospital. Jacob Wipf and David Hofer were sent to solitary confinement and placed on a starvation diet. They were made to stand nine hours each day with hands tied and stretched through the prison bars, their feet barely touching the floor.

Wipf managed to send a telegram to the wives of the two Hofer men who were hospitalized, and the women boarded the earliest train. The depot agent insisted that the telegram had come from Fort Riley rather than from Fort Leavenworth, and issued tickets to the wrong destination. After losing a day, the women arrived at midnight to find their husbands near death. When they returned in the morning, Joseph was dead. The guards refused Maria permission to see the dead body. She talked to the colonel, pleading in tears to see her husband's body. She was taken to the casket only to find that the body of her husband had been dressed in the military uniform he had so adamantly refused to wear. Michael Hofer died several days later. The wives and a few other relatives accompanied the bodies to their home community, where enormous funerals seared the Hutterite minds with the price of true apostolic faith.

The above accounts illustrate not only the uncompromising loyalty of the Hutterites to their community and to their religious faith, but also the reality of the conflict produced by their dualistic world. The two Hutterites who were faithful to their death, like their contemporaries, were prepared to die. Their culture prepared them to expect hostility in life. Death is a release from a "valley of tears," just as it is a release from a world that has rejected their concept of the good life.

VIEW OF THE EGO AND THE RELATION OF THE SEXES

In the Hutterite view, the individual will must be broken. This is achieved early, primarily during the kindergarten age, and is reinforced continually until death. In place of self-fulfillment there must be self-denial. The individual must be humble and submissive. After approximately twenty years of intensive indoctrination, the individual is expected to accept voluntarily the teachings of the colony. When he is able to express the remorse, abasement, and loathing associated with his sinful self, he will receive baptism. Individual identity must be fused with the community. Just as a grain of wheat loses its identity in the making of a loaf of bread (Rideman 1950:86), so the individual must lose his identity in one corporate body. "God worketh only in surrendered men."

Self-surrender, not self-development, is the Hutterite goal. The communal will, not the individual will, becomes important. The good of the majority governs the stages of life from birth to death. Since human nature is sinful from birth, Hutterites value education as a means for "planting" in children "the knowledge and the fear of God," not for self-improvement. The consequences of original sin are moderated by intensive teaching from an early age. "We should let the Heavenly Gardener implant such fruit that will bear everlasting life. The child's will should not be fulfilled, but the Father's will. Our will should be locked in His will."

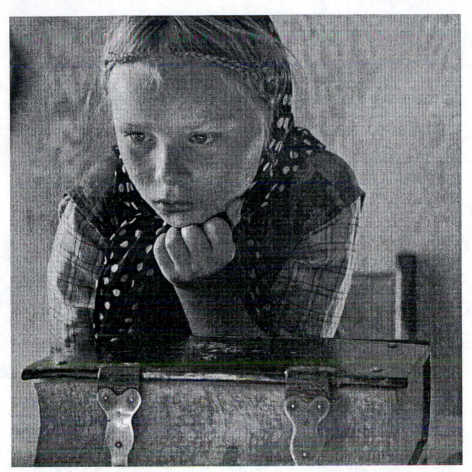

"We teach obedience first, then the faith."

Although the individual is "grafted into the divine character or nature" (Rideman 1950:18), he is never free from temptation of his carnal nature. His security in the divine order depends not on his verbal affirmation or the rite of baptism, but on his "proven works" or daily behavior. Behaviorally, this means adherence to the rules of the church community. The individual may not conform to his own interpretation of the "word" or his own notion of obedience. Since "God worketh in surrendered men," the individual must submit to the will of the community because community is the will of God.

The individual must never pray "My" Father but "Our" Father. Thus, one prays for the common good of the majority and not for the good of the individual. Since the community is the body of Christ, God dwells in the community.

The individual has a proper, defined place in the community. By divine order, male is over female, husband over wife, older over younger, and parent over child. Women have no formal vote or formal participation in church decisions. Marital relationships proceed from the divine order. God rules over the soul or spirit, the spirit rules over the body, and man rules over woman. As a woman should obey the man, so also the body should obey the spirit. In creation man has lordship over woman, while the woman has "weakness, humility, and submission." Woman should "heed her husband . . . and do all things with and naught without his counsel." If she does not, she forsakes the order of God. Man "should have compassion on the woman as the weaker instrument" and must care for her in temporal and spiritual things.

The purpose of marriage is to instruct and lead men to God. If the marriage is not rightly regarded and observed, "it leadeth men away from God and bringeth death." A husband must be head of only one wife, as Christ is the head of only one church. A marital union can be broken by transgression of the marriage promise, and if the husband "as the glory of God" dishonors himself through the weakness of the flesh, he breaks the union. A broken promise by either partner does not lead to divorce; reconciliation is possible only through repentance and restoration of the broken covenant. To achieve marriage "one should ask not his flesh but the elders that God might show" through the community "what God has provided from the beginning." Man and woman come together not through their own action and choice, but in accordance with God's will and order, and in fact, obedience to God and community are above obedience to spouse. Thus, if one partner forsakes the faith, the other remains bound to the community (Hutterian Brethren, 1987:286–293).

Physical attractiveness is a secondary consideration in marriage, while the primary factors are those which benefit the colony as a whole, namely, whether the girl is a good housekeeper, likes children, is obedient to the colony, and whether the boy shows initiative in his assigned work and accepts the values of the colony.

VIEW OF COMMUNITY AND OF PROPERTY

Living communally is believed to be the divine order of God, who from the beginning created all things for common use. Through private possession, it was man who brought disorder into the world by his grasping and greedy spirit. The dichotomy between the carnal and the spiritual is expressed in the right use of material goods. Carnal men are viewed as living in perpetual covetousness by making property, food, land, and "created things" the object of private gain. The sun, moon, day, air, and material things are for the good of all men, and to make them private property is to ignore God's order. "Therefore, whosoever will cleave to Christ and follow him must forsake such things." Just as the Father and the Son in Heaven live in common, and hide nothing from each other, so his children should also live (Rideman 1950:88–90).

God's "gifts are not given to one member alone, but for the whole body with its members." "The communion of saints must show itself not only in the spiritual but in temporal things also." "Through such wrong taking and collecting of created things he hath been led so far from God that he hath even forgotten the Creator." Privately owned material possessions lead human beings away from God. In his carnal state of mind man honors "created things" instead of making them subject to him (Rideman 1950:88).

Honest manual labor, making what is useful "for the benefit and daily use of man" is honorable, but merchandising (buying and selling for profit, without the contribution of labor) is a "sinful business" (Rideman 1950:112, 127). Material goods, as well as capital earnings, are for the welfare and benefit of the community. Every member "shall give and devote all his or her time, labor, services, earnings, and energies to . . . the community, freely, voluntarily, and without compensation. . . ." (Hutterian Brethren Church, Constitution, 1950). The individual, in turn, together with his dependents, are "supported, instructed, and educated" by the community.

The community is more important than the individual and governs the activity of the individual, and the corporate group has the power to exclude and to punish, to forgive and to readmit. The German teacher is charged with the formal instruction of the young and he is their primary disciplinarian. The father, as head of a family, supports the discipline of the colony, and the colony can require him to punish his own child in the presence of the group. The older person is required to correct the younger, regardless of the relationship, and self-assertion by the individual against the group is not permitted. The duties of each person are assigned by the community, and tasks may not be chosen or positions aspired to by the individual. Disobedience to the community means forsaking the commandment of God, and sin must be punished in proportion to its severity. Unconfessed sins will be held against the individual on the day of judgment and punishment will be meted out in the afterlife.

LANGUAGE AND REALITY

Hutterites view the world through Germanic-language thought patterns and from a perspective common to medieval Europe before the dawn of modern science. For them the word of God is contained in the German language, and since the word of God is believed to be eternal, the language forms and style of thinking convey symbolic spiritual meaning. Due to limited contact with other language groups, including other German-speaking people, and isolation from changes in intellectual thought, a type of pre-Lutheran language pattern and logic permeates their social patterns. The lack of interest in changing the destiny of history and of controlling nature through critical and scientific logic are distinctive of their view of the world.

Hutterites are trilingual, but have limited ability in three languages. The mother tongue of all Hutterites is a household dialect similar to that still spoken in certain parts of Austria, South Tyrol, and Bavaria. The child learns limited High German from biblical and religious sources in the German school. A speaking knowledge of English is acquired by all Hutterites in the English school. German and English usage are symbolic of the two kingdoms, the colony and the world. High German is used for all sacred and ceremonial occasions, and the sermons read in church have been copied from seventeenth-century German texts. "We believe," said a preacher, "that our faith can be expressed more deeply, sharply, and full in the German language."

The rigid character of the German sentence structure is supportive of the absolutism of the authority patterns. Language binds the thoughts of its speakers by the patterns of its grammar. For the Hutterites the supremacy of the German language is illustrated by their sermons. The words "scripture" and "sermon" are interchangeable in Hutterite usage. When a Hutterite preacher wants to know the interpretation of a biblical passage, he will rely on his old sermon books. Sermons are the unchallenged source of authority, and no individual, not even a preacher, may interpret the Bible without the aid of the traditional sermons. They say "No one among us is spiritual enough today to preach without the written sermons; it would be very unsafe." Preachers do not embellish their sermons with contemporary illustrations, as this would "distract us from the word of God." This dedication to the Gothic German handwritten sermons insulates the ideology from competing outside influences. Critical scholarship is considered unnecessary, for such scientific-individualistic conceptions militate against the wisdom of consensus.

When several Hutterite men were serving jail sentences as conscientious objectors during World War II, the authorities forbade them the use of their German books. Friends volunteered to translate their hymns and sermons into English, but when the elders examined the translations they declared that the meaning had been so watered down as to be worthless. The identification with the German language is so strong that the traditional Gothic printed type is equated with the sacred. The hymnal and school books, when reprinted by outside firms, must remain in Gothic typeface. Hutterite handwriting, too, employs the script alphabet, and not the so-called "English" (Latin) alphabet now commonly used in modern Germany. The unchanged form of words, phrases, and sentences is an example of the power of Holy Writ. Parallels in other cultures are Hebrew of the Old Testament, Arabic of the Koran, and, formerly, Latin in the Roman Catholic Mass, as well as Zuni ritual poetry when memorized "word perfect" and unchanged.

Private interpretation of the word of God is forbidden. No individual Hutterite, no matter how mystical or saintly his behavior, has legitimate authority to interpret the word of God. For the Hutterites there is no "inner light" to challenge either the word of God or the religious tradition of the community. The decaying Bibles and sermon books are placed in the casket of a deceased person. There, the pages of the worn-out book and the body decay, but the word of God and the soul are identified with the eternal and live forever.

Verbal sharing is very important to the colony and supportive of the communal social organization. Although the Hutterites are literate and capable of writing in both German and limited English, literacy is less important to them than verbal sharing. Oral sharing of words and phrases in ceremonial practices lends strong support to uniformity of thought patterns and communitarian values. In all colony schools from kindergarten through the rite of baptism, words and phrases are memorized and repeated in unison. All memorize the same or similar prayers, the same hymns, and the same vows. The right hymns must be sung in the right way "for the glory of God"; they must not be sung in a manner to make a "sweet sound" or for "carnal joy." Ritualization of prayers before and after meals, before retiring and when rising, are always considered necessary. A Hutterite is so thoroughly conditioned to ritual at mealtime and at coffee time that his hands form a prayer posture spontaneously before and after eating, whether the place is the dining hall, his apartment, or a roadside restaurant. Thus, access to God, to food, to sleep and to a new day is found through stylized prayer recited in the proper way. Individual fulfillment is achieved by fusion with the group in daily recitation and singing and in the evening church service. The blending of words and phrases with the communal whole allows little place for individual assertion, and individual utterances are undistinguishable from the whole. In

Always before and after eating, Hutterites fold their hands and give thanks.

verbal sharing, as in property ownership, the individual's voice is blended and fused into that of the group.

In a society that permits no material object to become sacred, special importance is attached to words, language patterns, and oral tradition; there are virtually no religious relics. Ritual centers around words, not objects or property. Bibles and sermon books are the most valued property, but the contents (the word) and not the material itself is believed to be holy. Even in baptism the word of God and not the water is holy. Passages from sacred writings are more easily shared than material objects, group recitation and singing being the most common forms of sharing. So intensive is the sharing that persons in the church service do not possess individual hymn books. Only the preacher has a book, and after reciting each line the group sings in unison.

The Hutterites have retained their medieval speech patterns for over four centuries even though they have borrowed expressions and words from countries in which they have lived. An analysis of their speech reveals a similarity to the languages of contemporary southern Bavaria and Austria, particularly the area of Carinthia, Austria. The southern Bavarian dialect is also spoken in parts of Tyrol, and a sprinkling of vocabulary reflects their stay in Slavic areas, Transylvania (Romania), Ukraine, and the United States. The terms for in-law relationships (*Schwiegermutter, sohn,* and so forth) reflect the pattern of Carinthia. The term for cucumber (*Kratsewets*) apparently entered the Hutterite speech pattern from Transylvania. From the Slavic languages there is *dšainik* for kettle, and from the Ukranian are the words for teapot (*căjink*) and cap (*xatıs*). The many English words used today by Hutterites center around technology and economic habits not common to them before their immigration to this country. English more than any other non-Germanic language has had the greatest influence on their vocabulary. On the whole there is a consistency in the traditional speech pattern with no observable changes in the ceremonial vocabulary. The Hutterites have synthesized a pre-Lutheran speech pattern with their doctrine so as to form a distinctive view of the world. This view has been supportive of their social organization for more than four centuries.

Before the evening meal, Hutterites gather to worship and give thanks. The place of worship is spacious, undecorated, and free of distractions. Each person has an assigned place.

SUMMARY OF WORLD VIEW

These existential postulates are the major ones professed by Hutterites. They provide individuals with cognitive guides to "reality." The manner in which professed beliefs are practiced varies a great deal from one society to another, and even within Hutterite society they vary in detail from one colony to another. The applications of the formal beliefs to the solutions of day-to-day living (normative postulates) will become clear in the chapters that follow.

As a corporate group who in a real sense are a minority culture strikingly different from populations surrounding them, the Hutterites have articulated many reasons for their separateness. The significance of birth, life, and death are determined by the culture, and knowledge of the Hutterite culture enables us to understand why from birth the people of that culture are believed to have the tendency to love carnal, personal pleasures, and how they manage to cope with a dual nature.

The Hutterite has the opportunity to change his destiny by giving up his individual will for the welfare of the community. This change in destiny requires a lifetime of submission to communal living in order to achieve the hope of eternal life after death. Death is managed in such a way that it becomes not a dreadful experience devoid of purpose, but the final triumphant step in restoration to a divine order.

The Hutterite world view includes the following:

1. Absolute authority resides in a single supernatural being, an omnipotent God, who created the universe and placed everything in a divine order and hierarchy. All events are ordered of God and nothing happens without the knowledge of God.
2. Through transgression of the divine order and the disobedience of man toward God, all nature became perverse. In its fallen or carnal state human nature desires self-recognition, self-ownership, and bodily (carnal) pleasure. Human nature is helpless and can never completely overcome the carnal tendency, and only by believing the word of God, by repentance, by receiving the grace of Christ, and through continual submission of the self to the will of God in communal living can the individual attain eternal life after death.
3. The carnal nature and the spiritual nature are inevitably antagonistic to each other and constitute two separate kingdoms. The fallen or carnal nature is displeasing to God; the spiritual nature permits an individual to be restored to the divine order where he will voluntarily share his life and his possessions.
4. The spiritual kingdom is ruled by the spirit of Christ and is known by the complete obedience experienced in sharing all material goods. Only in a divinely created fellowship, separated from the world, can men succeed in living communally, and only in this way can God be properly honored, worshipped, and obeyed.
5. At all times the individual must be submissive to the will of God that is explicitly manifested in the believing community. Self-surrender and not self-development is the divine order. Humans are endowed with both a carnal and a spiritual nature. They can overcome their carnal tendency by submission to the community and with the help of all the members.
6. All persons are born in sin and with a tendency toward evil and self-pleasure. This tendency can be modified by teaching young children the divine discipline. Children must be taught to be obedient to the "law" of their elders and superiors until they accept the mature discipline of the believing community.
7. Male dominance is reflected in the creation of the universe and is embodied in the relationships between the sexes and in marriage. Man is the leader in righteousness and in example. The divine order requires that woman be submissive and obedient to man.

8. Ultimate good is achieved in life only by surrender of the individual will to the will of God as manifest in the believing community where all material goods and spiritual gifts are shared in common. Only by living in the "ark of safety" can the individual overcome the selfish desires of his carnal tendency and be confident of eternal life after death.

CONCEPTS UNIQUE TO THE CULTURE

From the discussion thus far it will be observed that a number of concepts are unique to the culture. Their distinctive meanings are essential to the presentation that follows. Among the distinctive concepts are the following:

Anabaptism: A religious movement of the sixteenth century that insisted on the practice of adult rather than infant baptism, and the belief in a voluntary church separate and distinct from the civil church government. The Anabaptists insisted on intensive sharing, the practice of simple living, self-sufficiency, and the refusal to serve in the military.

Bruderhof: The domestic group with its buildings and physical complex required to carry on the activities of communal living. It is the local biologic, economic, ceremonial, and self-sustaining unit, and is synonymous with "colony."

Community (Gemeinsam or *Gemeinschaft):* The practice of owning and sharing material goods in common, with each individual working according to his ability and receiving according to his need. The practice of "community of goods" *Gütergemeinschaft)* is contrasted with individual ownership of material goods.

Carnal nature: See "spiritual nature."

Gemein: The church, a corporate spiritual and ceremonial group comprised of adult, baptized members of the community through whom the will of God is made manifest. Only men are eligible for church office, and only they are represented in the formal decisions made by the church.

Leut: The word "people," used as a suffix by Hutterites to distinguish the three administrative and endogamous groups of Hutterites: *Schmied-Leut, Darius-Leut,* and *Lehrer-Leut. Welt-Leut* or "worldly people" is also used to distinguish outsiders from Hutterites.

Order of God or *divine order:* The proper relationship established by God among all "created things." Man's place in the divine order determines all his relationships.

Ordnungen: The written rules of the community reflecting the will of God as made manifest through the community for particular times and situations.

Self-denial or *self-surrender (Gelassenheit):* Voluntarily renouncing individual will and accepting the will of God as made manifest in the sacred writings and as interpreted and required by the colony.

Sin: Behavioral disobedience to the will of God as revealed in the sacred writings and in the rules of community living as contextually defined by the colony. Sin is present from birth and is prone to be committed by the individual. Punishment for sin must be willingly accepted by the individual. A whole colony can sin by going against the rules and counsel of the preacher-assembly.

Spiritual nature: The unchanging, eternal, character of God, in contrast to *carnal nature* or *human nature,* which is earthly, corporeal, self-indulgent, sinful, evil, and displeasing to God.

Temporal: The transitory and passing nature of created and material things. By contrast, the *eternal* is the never-ending and spiritual aspect of creation, including man's soul, the word of God, and God.

Word of God: The revealed will of God in the sacred writings, especially the New Testament, as supported by the moral instructions in the Old Testament and the Apocrypha, which when believed and obeyed will enable persons to receive the spiritual nature. Obedience to the word of God enables the individual to subdue the carnal nature and to conform voluntarily to the order of God in communal living.

Worldly (Weltlichkeit) or *worldly people (Welt-Leut):* The noncolony people who live in disobedience to God and serve the earthly or carnal nature that every person possesses from birth.

2 / Colony Life Patterns

It is Saturday evening. Everyone is outside their apartments on the village green between the longhouses and the kitchen enjoying the summer twilight. The center of the colony is alive with activity. Some of the older people are sitting on folding chairs and talking; a grandfather has a baby on his lap, a grandmother is knitting. Several young parents are bathing their preschool children in tubs set on the door step, where the splashing overflow waters the flowers and washes the steps. The shop mechanic, who repaired a tractor after supper during this rush agricultural period, is scrubbing his feet in a tub by his apartment while the babysitter, his young sister-in-law, carries warm water to him. The school children dash and play leapfrog. Some young people wander around. A young boy sitting on his heels is teasing a small cluster of girls, and in retaliation one girl knocks off his hat and another pushes him off balance. There is constant movement and friendly exchange. As it grows dark, the babies are put to bed, the old people go to sleep, then the school-age children and the parents of young children retire. Finally, the young people return to their family apartments and the colony is quiet until sunrise.

The Hutterite view of the world is given concrete expression within the boundaries of the colony. As is common with religion in all cultures, the Hutterites "desire to live in a pure and holy cosmos, as it was in the beginning, when it came fresh from the Creator's hand" (Eliade, 1961:65). They believe that this cosmos can be achieved only within a Hutterite colony, for only within a colony can God's order be maintained. The concept of order influences the spatial patterns of the colony; the buildings must be in proper relationship to one another and squared with the compass. Temporal patterns reflect a right order for all activity. Social patterns reflect a right order, for everyone must have the right position in a hierarchical world.

There is a circular reinforcement: The world view of the Hutterites leads to the creation of an environment that is ordered spatially, temporally, and socially. It is within this created environment that the individual Hutterite matures and ages, which in turn reinforces a belief in a divinely created, orderly world. For the Hutterites, the colony, where order has become synonymous with eternity and godliness, is the center of the universe. The colony is believed to be an expression of the divine plan, and is compared to the ark of Noah in the biblical account of the flood. The people whom God selected to be in the ark were those who were worshipping him correctly. Only those in the ark (the colony) are safely prepared to escape the judgment of God and to receive eternal life. As one preacher explained, "you either are in the ark, or you are *not* in the ark."

SPATIAL PATTERNS

Dariushof is a colony located on the northern edge of the Great Plains about one hundred miles from a large trading center and ten miles from a small town which is their post office. The colony is sufficiently near to its parental colony (fifteen miles) so that work and services can be exchanged, but not near enough so that young people can walk between colonies. The colony buildings (numbering about fifty) are reached by a gravel road and cannot be seen from the public road nearby. This colony owns 6,000 acres and leases 3,000 additional acres, which is about the average for lands owned or leased by other colonies in the area.

Although there is no Hutterite style of architecture, there is a characteristic layout. The center of the colony is the kitchen complex and the longhouses or living houses, with their associated sheds and the kindergarten. The longhouses run due north and south, for as a preacher put it: "They are squared with the compass. You don't walk crooked to the earth, you walk straight; that is how our buildings should be, straight with the compass and not askew." Typically, each longhouse has four apartments, each with a separate entrance. A normal-sized apartment has three rooms. There is an entrance room containing a table, straight chairs, a wash basin, a cupboard for a few dishes, and the stairway entrance to the attic; off either side of the entrance room is a bedroom with two double beds, one or two day beds, and a crib. The second story of the house is one long, unpartitioned attic in which the families store their out-of-season clothing and tools. The newer houses have basements. The many other buildings in a colony are laid cut parallel or at right angles to the longhouses.

Shown here is a newly established colony. At center is the communal kitchen surrounded by longhouses. The kindergarten and school buildings are on the left. The repair shop is in the foreground.

All the people over six years of age meet in the kitchen three times a day to eat their meals. Here the women work preparing food for the colony, launder their family's clothes, and the colonists come to bathe or shower. Outside the kitchen is the bell that signals mealtime, announces that the women must come to work, or that calls for help should there be a fire.

Ideally, the color of the buildings reflects the use of the building or the attitude of the people toward the building. In one colony the kitchen, the longhouses, and the kindergarten are all painted white with blue trim. The small buildings near the long-houses that are primarily for colony use, such as the bee house, the shoe shop, and the small traditional goose houses, are also painted white with blue. In contrast, those buildings used primarily for economic activity that brings in money from the outside economy are painted, in this particular colony, a bright red. They include the machine shop, the pump house, the root cellar, and various barns. An exception is the public school house, which in *Dariushof* is stucco instead of wood, is painted yellow, is oriented to face the state road rather than the colony, and from which the sign giving its former name and school district has never been removed. Although physically part of the colony, the English school is placed to one side. The kindergarten and the German school are completely embraced within the colony.

The spatial orientation of the buildings and the unified color scheme reflect Hutterite thinking: everything is classified; each part of the universe has its correct place, which in turn determines its correct function and proper use. "By their fruits ye shall know them" is interpreted to mean that one's appearance reflects one's attitude or the strength of one's belief. Or, more succinctly, as one strict minister said when discussing the dress of the women of his colony, "I don't care how frilly and frothy their underwear is, it's what shows that counts." What shows classifies the woman, just as it classifies the building. Her dress indicates that she is: (1) an adult woman, (2) a Christian, (3) a Hutterite, and (4) that she knows her position relative to men. It also shows whether she is dressed for work, for evening church, or for Sunday.

Hutterites consider life in this world to be transient and temporary, and where it is lived is of no consequence, for they are always "in strange lands under Jews and Gentiles." In these strange lands they create their own physical environment which is remarkably uniform. The colony is the concrete expression of the Hutterite belief system and the social environment in which the beliefs are transmitted to the children. What gives a Hutterite identity is not the place he or she has lived, nor having lived in one or many places, but rather that in spite of geographic moves the pattern of life has always been the same, even to the floor plan of his house and the position of his home relative to that of his neighbors. A specific place is not important—specific orientation is of utmost importance.

The diagram of a recently formed colony (*Starhof,* p. 24) illustrates how new spatial patterns are fused with the old. This colony was founded in 1991 with eighty-one persons. The longhouses are arranged in a circular pattern, with the church and school occupying the center of the community. The absence of a kindergarten building is atypical. Industry, shops, and livestock are not a part of the circular pattern. All the colony buildings except for five of the living houses reflect the traditional orientation to the points of the compass.

The colony owns 4,000 acres. No acreages are rented or irrigated. The economy is based on agricultural production: wheat, 1,000 acres; barley, 1,200; flax, 800; and

Starhof Colony 1991. The circular arrangement of the long houses is innovative.

rape-seed, 800 acres. Specialization is reflected in the economy. There are no cattle, sheep, goats, or horses. Poultry and hogs are the main sources of income. Sows number 380, and the colony expects to market 4,000 hogs annually. There are 9,000 laying hens yielding 7,400 eggs daily.

The newly formed colony is ultramodern with several computers. Each apartment has a telephone and is equipped with a variety of modern appliances including an automatic dishwasher, various small electrical appliances, and bathrooms equipped with showers and tubs. The apartments are heated with electricity. Every household has access to the basement, and as in most other colonies, there is a wine cellar. Instead of the traditional bell that summons people to the dining hall, there is an electronic buzzer.

COMMUNAL TIME PATTERNS

Hutterite theology teaches that there is a right order for every activity. Consequently, time functions to organize Hutterite activities and social relationships. The daily schedule involving all the members of the colony is severely patterned. The weekly schedule builds up to a climax in the Sunday complex, preparing for Sunday. The liturgical calendar is integrated with the change of seasons and the agricultural cycle. Most women's work is organized by a time schedule, and their family work follows daily, weekly, and seasonal patterns. Their colony work is of two types: general food preparation and cleaning that is performed by the women working together in a group, and the rotating jobs for which one or two women assume responsibility for one week at a time.

Within this small face-to-face society, time spent on earth functions as an impartial means for establishing order in social relationships. The individuals are ranked by age and sex; age determines both the group to which an individual belongs and, generally, his place within the group. The stages of life do not correspond simply to biological phases but represent social functions.

Age Sets

Age sets are as follows:

House children: birth to two years. The small child who is still fed at home is referred to as a house child.

Kindergarteners: three to five years. The child in this age set attends the *Klein-Schul* or kindergarten. Some colonies will admit the child to kindergarten at the age of two-and-one-half years.

School children: six to fourteen years. These children attend the *Gross-Schul* or German school, and they also attend the public or English school from the time they are approximately six until the day before they are fifteen. At age fifteen the child enters the adult dining room.

Young people: age fifteen to baptism. This age sometimes has been called "the in-between years," or "the foolish years." Foolish does not imply any juvenile delinquency, but that the person is immature and sometimes wavering in his loyalties. Boys of this age are given the most challenging physical labor; girls do most of the colony painting.

Baptism (about age twenty) to marriage: Baptism signifies membership in the colony and is usually followed rather closely by marriage.

Marriage and adulthood: Following marriage the adult man is eligible for leadership positions, such as German teacher, chickenman, or shop foreman. After he has proved himself in these categories, he becomes eligible for an executive position by being elected to the council. Adult women's work increases with the number of her children; all the clothing and bedding is produced for the family within the family unit. Certain nonrotating jobs for women are related to their husband's work assignment. The "sick people's" cook is usually the wife of the cattleman. The German school mother is frequently the wife of the German school teacher. The head cook is also assigned that position by the council, but the assignment is not necessarily related to her husband's job.

Aged: The older men gradually retire from their leadership positions but remain advisers and interpreters of tradition. The older women admonish the young people, distribute the colony allotments to individual families, and help care for the babies.

Although the age sets are distinct in the life cycle, one concept may overlap several stages. For example, a child is considered a baby until he or she hits back, until the next one is born, until entering kindergarten, and until entering German school. A person becomes an adult through a series of stages: when he or she begins eating with the adults at fifteen, when baptized, when married, and when the first child is born. These age groups are discussed in greater detail in the chapter on socialization.

Religious thought in traditional and preliterate cultures has conceived of two classes of time—the sacred and the secular. The Hutterites participate in both of these realms. Sacred time is related to the beliefs about creation and is nonflowing, that is, it is eternal, and pertains to God, who is believed to be without beginning or end. It also is characteristic of the word of God, for God's words always remain an inseparable part of God and therefore are eternal. The Hutterite soul has a beginning but no end.

Secular time is the measure of events that take place on earth, which have both a beginning and an end. It applies to all material objects, including the human body.

Intermediate between sacred and secular time are history and dreams. For the Hutterites, history is important as a dimension of the presence of God in the world. They are not interested in history in terms of dates on a secular time scale but as steps in the development of the church of God. Therefore, historical events that are unrelated to their own outlook on life are of little meaning to them and even their own history is remembered as it strengthens their faith rather than as a dated sequence of events. This means that there is some fusion of the beginning of Christianity (the historical period of Christ's birth and the writing of the Bible) with the beginning of the Hutterites (during the persecutions of the sixteenth and seventeenth centuries and the writing of the Hutterite sermons). Miracles of the sixteenth century may be mixed with those of the nineteenth, for the worldly date is unimportant compared with the fact that God "broke into history." History is a dimension of secular time that is recalled primarily because it illustrates eternity. Dreams are also intermediate between secular and sacred time. Unlike activities in secular time that should pass quickly and that one does not wish to extend, a Hutterite may report that he did not want to "leave that dream." Occasionally, dreams may be equated with visions and then, too, they are outside the secular time scale.

Almost every evening, between the end of the day's work and the evening meal, secular time on the colony is interrupted by sacred time. The total community of school children and adults gathers together for the evening church service. Here they symbolically return to the time of their origin. The daily renewal of motivation through ritual participation is of utmost importance. For the Hutterite it is the sacred time which makes secular time meaningful. As the preacher slowly reads the sermons, unhurriedly recites the prayers, and the congregation sings the long, slow hymns, time is suspended: there is no rush to complete this task, for the members are participating in a nonsecular time dimension. God's time is eternal, nonflowing, sacred.

In the daily round of meals and work the Hutterites are keenly aware of the passage of time. The day is broken into small units of time that form a tight, although not rigid, schedule. This severe patterning means that the individual members of the colony have little free choice and few decisions to make with regard to time. Just as material objects are not owned by a Hutterite, he also has little concept of private time. Time is not something that can be reserved for private use; it is not equated with money. The time that is needed for the completion of an operation, for example, the building of a feed shed, is considered, but not the time given by the various contributing individuals. However, the speed with which an individual works gives status. A woman will always know how long it took her to make an article of clothing, and both adults and children set up tasks in such a way that the speed with which they are finished is obvious. There is little savoring of the moment, for the attitude toward almost everything in this earthly life is to get it over with. This applies to meals, to work, even to life itself, which is believed to be short, transitory, and of real significance only as it relates to eternal time.

Daily Schedule

The *daily schedule* involves all members of the colony, and the patterns of all individuals mesh in such a way that the colony runs smoothly and efficiently. The basic schedule varies with the time of year; it is modified in accord with the weather on a given day and is adjusted slightly to accommodate special tasks or an emergency. Thus, in winter when the daylight hours are few and there is less agricultural work, the rising bell rings later (at 7:00 A.M. instead of 6:15 A.M.) and supper is earlier (at 6:15 P.M. instead of 7:00 P.M.). If it rains during haying season, the rising bell may ring at 7:00 A.M. instead of 6:15 A.M. because the hay is too wet to cut. When the men are busy haying, food is sent out to the fields to them and they are fed supper when they return for the night, which may be as late as 10:00 P.M. If the women are not finished with their colony work, supper may be served late for all the adults in order that the task may be completed before the meal. When colony work is pressing, the evening church service is omitted.

Each age set has its own daily schedule. Most adults are up an hour or more before the rising bell. The time of rising is determined by their special work assignments and the age and number of their children. The woman who is baking mixes the bun dough at 3:30 A.M., the cowman starts milking at 4:30 A.M., the mother of a young baby nurses him at 5:00. At 6:15 the rising bell rings, and at 6:30 the bell for adult breakfast is sounded. At 6:45 the school children eat breakfast, and the three- to six-year-olds go to the kindergarten for their breakfast. After eating, the school girls clean the dining room and kitchen. Before the children's breakfast the women clean the adult dining room, wash the dishes, and gather food to carry back to the house children, whom they feed in the apartments. The men do their chores, and the unassigned men and boys assemble informally to learn their job assignments for the morning. The work bell for the women rings any time between 7:15 and 8:50, depending on the amount of colony work. About 9:00 A.M. the adults and any children working with them pause at their places of work for a snack of a cool drink or coffee with buns. At 10:00 A.M. the bell rings to announce dinner for the kindergarten children and the house children. Dinner is brought to the kindergarten, and the three- to six-year-olds are fed by the kindergarten mother, who then puts them to sleep. Mothers carry food

Adult men and women eat at separate tables in the colony dining hall. Age determines the seating.

home for their house children, feed them, and put them to bed. At 11:00 the bell rings for the school children's dinner. At 11:30 the warning bell rings to remind the men to get ready for dinner. At 11:45 the dinner bell rings, and all the adults eat their main meal, seated at their assigned places, the men on one side of the room, the women on the other, arranged around the tables according to age. Afterward the women wash the dinner dishes, the adults rest, and then have a light snack. After the snack the men return to work, and sometime between 1:30 and 2:30 the work bell rings signaling the women's return to the kitchen for colony work. At 3:00 P.M. the kindergarten children are fed a snack, recite their prayers, and go home about 3:30. At 5:00 the mothers carry food back to the apartments and feed their house children and kindergarten children. At 6:00 the bell rings for the school children's supper. At 6:30 the school children and all the adults assemble for the daily church service. The adults eat at 7:00. After the meal area is cleaned and the men have finished the evening chores, the members of the colony are free to talk, visit, or work on individual projects until it is time to give the children a snack, supervise their prayers, and put them to bed. It is a schedule that keeps everyone busy, but unhurried. Time seems to pass quickly, partly because the day is divided into such small blocks of time.

The colony bell is rung to announce rising time and most of the meals; it is rung to call the women to work or to announce a wedding shivaree; its ring summons the members to help put out a fire or cope with an emergency. The bell pertains to worldly events that involve large segments of the community. Unimportant details like snacks are not signaled by the bell, nor does the bell ring for a meal that is served directly after a church service, for the colony is already together and it would be superfluous to ring it. The bell is never used to call the members to church, as is the custom among "worldly" people. If there is a question about whether there will be a church service, children are sent around to inform the families. When the minister

The colony bell summons people to work and to the dining hall.

starts to the service, the others follow. Church services are of a different order of importance from regular temporal activities; this supremely important gathering of the entire community is never announced by the bell.

Weekly Schedule and Sunday Complex

The weekly pattern of activity builds to a climax in preparation for Sunday. The men are caught up in the Sunday complex only on Friday and Saturday, but the women's work and the food served follows a traditional weekly schedule. On Monday the women do the family washing at the community wash house at a time assigned to them. They wash in rotation, beginning with the oldest woman and ending with the youngest, moving up one turn each week. Ideally, a woman does all the washing for her family and finishes the ironing and the mending on Monday. This is possible if she is fortunate enough to wash early that week and if there is no colony work in the afternoon. A colony may mildly boast that everyone is finished washing before 10:30 Monday morning. In some colonies the women try to polish their floors every day, but if they are unable to do this, they always polish them on Tuesdays and Fridays. During the summer the school girls pick peas for the kitchen on Tuesday morning. On Wednesday, Thursday, and Friday the women hoe the garden and pick vegetables. Women with small children wash again on Thursday. Friday is a major cleaning day. The kitchen and dining room cement floors are scrubbed with hot water and soap by all the women. The women clean their own apartments and wax and polish their floors. The cook, the baker, and the milking woman clean their respective work areas because women's work assignments change on Sunday night and they want to leave their places of work clean. One of the work teams makes

A girl washes the German school towels in the large laundry equipment.

noodles. Saturday morning all the women roll buns, and the unmarried girls scrub the school house so it will be ready for the Sunday church services. On Saturday afternoon everyone bathes, hair is combed, and beards are trimmed. Everything and everyone must be clean for Sunday.

There is a weekly pattern for the food. In *Dariushof* during the summer months bread is baked on Monday and Wednesday; rolls are baked on Saturday, and on

Tuesday, from before seeding until after harvest, when the boys are working hard, a treat is baked for the people to eat in their homes. The meals have a pattern that varies somewhat with the season and varies considerably from one colony to another. The sweetened orange pekoe tea that is served at Saturday supper is called "Saturday tea" to distinguish it from the medicinal or herbal teas that are drunk in the homes. A person with stomach trouble may regularly skip a certain meal because he knows that the food to be served does not agree with him. Sunday dinner consists of noodle soup and roast duck or, if there is no duck, chicken or goose.

Sunday begins with the Saturday evening church service. Among the *Darius-Leut* the women and girls wear special Saturday afternoon dresses to this service and to supper. Saturday evening everyone sings hymns informally and visits, discussing religion and retelling Hutterite history. People try to go to bed early on Saturday night so they will not be tired for Sunday. Sunday morning the waking bell rings late at 7:30. The women wear nice dresses to Sunday breakfast, the school children wear clean clothes to breakfast, and the kindergarteners, because they do not attend church, wear regular clothes. The kindergarten children are often cared for during this time by one of the school children so that the kindergarten teacher will be free to attend church. After breakfast the women and girls change into Sunday clothes and at 9:00 go to the service wearing dresses that are worn only for church. The sermons delivered were written during periods of persecution when the Hutterites were becoming a distinct people; they are not spontaneous or intellectual lectures on contemporary concerns. Even the rhythm of the preacher's voice differs from ordinary speech during this period of suspended temporality. The function of the sermons is not only to interpret the meaning of Biblical passages, but to guide the Hutterites through the present, secular "evil times."

When church is over at approximately 10:30, the women and girls change into Sunday afternoon dresses and everyone proceeds immediately to Sunday dinner. After dinner the adults take a long Sunday afternoon rest. At 1:30 P.M. the unbaptized members of the colony assemble with the German teacher for Sunday school. Here they demonstrate how well they have listened to the morning sermon and recite the hymn verses they have had to memorize during the week. Families are together Sunday afternoon; there is some visiting within the colony, and if another colony is within easy traveling distance, there will often be an exchange of visits, with the visitors attending Sunday evening church (4:30) and supper (5:15) at the host colony. Weekdays are fairly uniform, but Sunday is a very different day. The leisurely Sunday schedule functions to distinguish this holy day from work days. In a Hutterite colony Sunday is long; the church service is long, the rest period is long, and there is almost no work done. Each person is reminded that God's time is measured by eternity, in strong contrast with the swift flow of hours during the busy work week.

Colonies vary in the strictness with which they observe Sunday. Some allow absolutely no unnecessary work, although none are puritanical in their definition of necessary. Other colonies are quite relaxed about observing Sunday and permit clothes to be washed, garden produce to be picked, and ducks to be plucked on Sunday afternoon. When the weather is unseasonable for harvesting during the week, a colony may decide to work in the fields on Sunday. The rule of no Sunday work that is so pervasive in many Christian denominations in America can be adjusted by the

Hutterites through a community decision made in the interest of the total colony. Since goods and time all belong to God, no individual is benefiting from Sunday work and God is still being honored.

Liturgical Calendar

The liturgical calendar punctuates the year and divides it into definable seasons. It begins with Advent (the preparation for the coming Christ) and ends with Pentecost (the establishment of the Christian Church) {Friedman 1965:158}. During the long and uneventful winter, events are placed by relating them to the liturgical calendar; during the busy agricultural season, events are usually related to the major agricultural activity. Pigs are butchered "between Three Kings Day and Easter," but the baker makes Tuesday treats "from before seeding till after harvest." The liturgical cycle and the agricultural cycle are interrelated. In addition to the universal Christian holidays of Christmas and Easter, there are special services that are performed at the correct time for the specific colony. The harvest sermon is read the Sunday after the harvest is gathered. Specific sermons are read to meet colony needs, such as discipline or comfort for the sick; otherwise, Hutterite preachers follow a traditional yearly pattern in selecting the sermon to be read aloud on a specific Sunday. Each of the two preachers keeps a record of the date and text of all sermons delivered, who read them, and the hymns that were sung. The liturgical pattern specifies the celebration of important Christian holidays, but it is sufficiently flexible to allow incorporation of sermons that celebrate significant colony events.

AUTHORITY PATTERNS

All authority both inside and outside the church is believed to originate with the supernatural. Governmental or secular authority is believed to have been ordained by God in his wrath to take vengeance on evil and to discipline the godless. Within the church there is order without physical coercion; baptized members are believed to have received the supernatural gift of the Holy Spirit through obedience and submission, and they have more power and responsibility than those who have not been baptized.

Bureaucratic Organization

All the baptized members of the colony make up the *Gemein* or church. The group, not individuals, has the power to exclude and to accept members. Women participate in the church service by being present and joining in the prayers and hymns, and by formally greeting newly baptized members, but they "have no voice" in church and therefore do not participate in formulating colony policy, nor are they eligible for church leadership positions. Only baptized men are eligible for the departmental positions such as cattleman, pigman, shop mechanic, shoemaker, and only they may vote to elect members to these positions and to decide the economic, social, and religious life of the colony.

Five to seven of the baptized men are elected to form the council. They hold the key positions in the colony, including those of first preacher, second preacher, house-holder, and field manager. Often the German school teacher and one or two other men who hold leadership positions in the colony or whose age entitles them to a position of authority serve on the council. The council functions as an executive committee and makes many decisions, such as who shall be allowed to go to town or to visit relatives. The council members initiate changes in the appointment of subordinate job and departmental positions, execute discipline, and perform a judicial function. The actions of the council are directed by the church and are neither performed in the name of God nor for God, but with the help of God. Although the first preacher has the highest leadership position, his actions are subject to review by the council. Authority is thus group-centered, and decisions are derived through unified and continuous decision making by the council members. The individual council member has learned to be submissive and has been taught that the individual never reaches a state of perfection. Ideally, group decisions are free from partiality and are regarded as a higher source of truth than those made by an individual.

The preacher receives no formal training prior to his election. He is elected by lot from nominations by his own colony (with the aid of other colony delegates). He is ordained to exercise full powers only after several years of proven leadership. A preacher must have the ability to be conservative in religious values but progressive in work and economic affairs. Good handwriting is an asset since he must transcribe the sermons. He must be able to exert authority wisely, since he is expected to carry out the collective will as well as God's will. His role encompasses total as well as specific responsibility. Ideally, he refers all weighty matters to the council. His religious duties include conducting church services and funerals as well as performing marriages and baptisms. He hears personal problems, voluntary confession, and administers punishment for sins. He must interpret the present in terms of the past. He must oversee the life-long indoctrination of his people and the spiritual tempo of the colony. He has a direct interest in seeing that the colony schools are functioning properly, but his relation to the teachers is informal. He has the responsibility for smoothing over difficulties that arise between members. He keeps a record of births, marriages, and deaths, which reflects concern for both their history and marital patterns, and he keeps travel records when members leave the colony for trips. The preacher is intimately concerned with the economic well-being of the colony. He keeps an eye on the activities of the householder to insure that the colony is run efficiently enough to provide for its people's needs and for future expansion. He also countersigns checks with the householder. The preacher is both guardian of traditions and spokesman for the colony in its "foreign affairs." He must remain ever vigilant against the *Weltgeist,* the spirit of the world.

The life history of the preacher of one colony reflects his intimate experience with every phase of colony life. He was born in South Dakota, the son of an assistant preacher, moved to Canada with the colony at the age of eleven. He is now in his fifth colony. In his youth he was a horseman, herding sheep and cattle and caring for a team of horses. He drove a big steam engine for plowing wheat stubble. In the summer he swam in the James River with his peers. Some of his schooling was obtained in South Dakota and some in Canada. School days ended at age fifteen when he was assigned the job of herding sheep with his uncle. For a whole summer he slept in a tent, caring for the sheep and guarding them from wild animals, especially coyotes. Another summer he broke six horses, maintained the harness for all colony horses, and helped keep the plows and cultivators in repair. For five successive winters he cared for 175 horses that were fed from straw piles. If any of his charges became diseased, he had to identify the animal and treat the ailment. At twenty-two he was married to the daughter of the householder; his wife was two years younger than he. Following marriage the colony branched, and he and his wife moved thirty miles away with the new colony. There he held three jobs simultaneously: pigman, horseman, and tanner. At thirty-one he was elected to succeed his father as German teacher. He taught thirty-seven pupils in German school on weekdays, and fifty-six pupils on Sunday. He was elected to the council at thirty-eight and at age forty was elected a preacher to assist his father-in-law, who was head preacher at that time. By the time he was forty-three years old the colony was large enough to branch again. He became the head preacher of the newly formed colony that was established four hundred miles away. Meanwhile, there was adverse legislation directed against the Hutterites and he, with a delegation of six preachers, represented their concerns before legislative committees on many occasions. Finally, when he was forty-six his colony once again voted to form another branch, this time fifteen miles away. His leadership tasks were multiple. In one year he made ten trips to other colonies to assist in ordaining preachers, to preach funeral sermons, and to mediate disputes. Two of these were extended "trouble-shooting" trips, in which the Elder of his *Leut* requested his services with six others to attend to disciplinary problems. In his lifetime he has helped to silence three preachers, two for excessive drinking and one for incompetency. He attends the preachers' conferences usually held twice annually and, in addition to his full duties in the colony, he reads Hutterite chronicles and binds sermon books during the winter months.

To summarize, the bureaucratic organization of the colony can be described briefly as follows:

1. *The colony,* or *Bruderhof.* The colony is a domestic group consisting typically of all persons of Hutterite parentage or persuasion residing on the premises. It is the biologic, economic, ceremonial, and self-sustaining unit within which the needs of its members are met through the activities of communal living.
2. *The church,* or *Gemein.* The church consists of all the baptized men and women. They celebrate communion as an exclusive unit and welcome back into their midst repentant members. Only baptized men may vote in formal decisions. They vote on major colony policies and determine who will hold positions of leadership.
3. *The council.* The council consists of five to seven men selected by the *Gemein* to serve as executives. The first minister, the assistant minister, the householder, and the field manager are always on the council. Sometimes one individual will hold two of these offices or there may be no assistant minister. Except in a small colony, these positions are usually represented by four different men. Generally one or two other department heads or older men also serve on the council. They sit in order of rank, facing the congregation. They make practical day-to-day decisions, grant permission for travel, judge minor disagreements, and help the colony to run efficiently by making many semiroutine decisions.
4. *The informal subcouncil.* The first minister (sometimes the assistant preacher), the householder, and the field manager generally meet after breakfast each day to lay out the day's work and assign men to the various jobs.

5. *The householder.* The householder is in a peculiar position, for, under the direction of the council and the *Gemein* and with the help of the department managers, he is responsible for the economic prosperity of the colony. In the economic sphere he represents the colony to the outside world. Outsiders generally call him "the boss."

6. *The head preacher.* The head preacher is responsible for all aspects of community life, both economic and, to a greater extent, moral. He must "shepherd his flock" and "keep his hive in order." He is directed in this all-inclusive role by his own colony *Gemein* and by the preachers of his *Leut,* who ordained him to his position and have the power to remove him should they see fit. He represents the community in all its aspects to the outside world and interprets the world to the colonists.

Male and Female Subcultures

Within the Hutterite colony two subcultures exist, that of the men and that of the women. Women are believed to be inferior to men intellectually and physically and to need direction, protection, guidance, and consideration. For while it is believed that man was molded in God's likeness, reflecting something of God's glory, woman was taken from man and has weakness, humility, and submission. "Women just *are* inferior." At the time of marriage the husband does not leave his colony; his bride is usually from another colony and must move into his and adjust to new people and a new life. The women do not formally participate in colony decisions nor do they select their own leaders. The man's work is assigned by the colony and is virtually unaffected by obligations to his family, except that married men do not work on the night shift during harvest and are expected to help their wives with rotating colony work if that work is heavy.

Although women do not participate in formal colony decisions as a group, they are relatively free to intervene when they or their families are affected. Women may never defend their position on the basis of being an individual, but must appeal to the welfare of the group. Such patterns of behavior can be observed with respect to the socialization of children. Hutterite youngsters who are punished by the German school teacher (always a male) seek and receive comfort from their mothers. When hurt physically, the children seek comfort from the father (the protector from the world and the environment). While the father tends to uphold the rules of the patriarchal system, due to his own involvement in the structure, his wife may be more lenient in her attitude and more critical of the punishment. Wives feel less restrained in making complaints, while husbands will try to avoid confrontation with the colony power structure. A husband would rather suffer unjustly than complain openly. A wife has little to lose by complaining, but she may be frustrated because her husband will not give her the support she wants. She often projects her annoyance and mildly dislikes men as a group. Women, as a group, support each other against masculine influence, and even a dominant female will receive the support of the weaker ones and vice versa. The cultures of men and women are different and at points are opposed. Psychologists have reported striking differences in the scores of Hutterite men and women on various personality tests (Kaplan and Plaut 1956:34–44).

The loyalties of the men are somewhat divided between their peer group (the colony power structure), their family of orientation, and their family of procreation. The women are primarily oriented toward their family of procreation and therefore are more difficult for the colony to manage and integrate—especially when this attitude is coupled with some antagonism toward the men. One preacher declared: "Our colony troubles would amount to very little if it were not for the women." Married women appear to have less identification with the colony than do the men. This is indicated by the fact that men (and boys) seldom complain about the hard work even when they are haying from 7:00 in the morning until 10:00 at night. But the women complain openly when they have too much colony work in one day.

Women's Work Patterns

Women's work patterns are described in the context of colony life patterns, for the women are less involved in economic competition with the outside-society. Certain women have nonrotating positions of responsibility assigned to them. The most influential position is that of head cook, and in those colonies in which a woman is the gardener the second most influential position is that of gardener. The tailoress is frequently the oldest active woman in the colony, and with the help of one or two elderly women, she divides the cloth and distributes clothing and tools among the colony members, keeping a record of what has been distributed. Generally, two older or unmarried women are assigned to care for the kindergarten. In some colonies there are three kindergarten mothers, and occasionally only one. The women alternate and are in charge of the kindergarten for one day at a time. In *Dariushof* the German mother is the wife of the German teacher, and the milkmaid is the wife of the cattleman. In some colonies the milkmaid also is the cook for convalescing members, especially new mothers; in other colonies the diet cook is a separate position.

With the exception of these positions, work roles for women rotate, with the change-over taking place on Sunday night. Basically, the schedule is arranged

Kitchens have stainless steel equipment.

according to age, but it becomes modified by childbirth, illness, visits away from the colony, and by time taken to care for a new mother. The two most responsible rotating jobs are cooking and baking. Women begin cooking and baking when they are seventeen years old and stop when they are aged forty-five or over. Other rotating jobs are helping in the milk house, cleaning up after meals, making noodles, and supervising canning. Women begin this work when they are fifteen and continue until they are forty-five or fifty. In addition to the rotating colony jobs there is general colony work that the women do as a group. This involves food preparation such as rolling buns, peeling potatoes, canning and freezing food, butchering chickens, ducks, and geese, and helping when pigs are slaughtered. The women help with food production by planting potatoes, unless this is a major crop, hoeing the garden, picking vegetables, and caring for ducklings and goslings. They also pluck ducks and geese to obtain feathers that are used both by the colony to make bedding and sold as a cash crop. The women help make the soap and clean the colony buildings; they scrub the kitchen at least once a week. Girls between the ages of fifteen and marriage do most of the colony scrubbing, all the painting and varnishing, and most of the fruit picking. Young people from several colonies may be taken to distant states or provinces to pick fruit for colony use. The expeditions are considered recreation leading to wider friendship and often courtship, even though they involve considerable work.

Work patterns for women are traditional but they are modified by informal consensus of the women under the direction of the head cook. They decide when there are enough women to divide into teams for dishwashing, potato peeling, and noodle making. It is they, and not the men, who allocate certain jobs to the unmarried girls. In addition to their colony work, women must keep their apartments in immaculate

Poultry for the market is processed and government-inspected on the colony.

order, make the clothing used by the members of their family, do the family washing, and feed and care for their house children. One woman with eight children made over one hundred articles of clothing during November and December. The pattern of family work can most easily be illustrated by describing the work of a specific woman on a winter Wednesday when she had no rotating colony assignment. In other words, this is the basic schedule of family work to which would be added the usual Monday washing, the work announced by the ringing of the colony bell, and the rotating assignment were it a week during which the woman was responsible for cooking or baking.

Katie is in her mid-thirties. She has six children who range in age from twelve years to eight months. Her day starts at 5:00 A.M. when she takes the infant into bed with her and nurses him. At 6:15 the alarm rings and she gets up, dresses, prays, and washes before waking her husband, who follows the same procedure. One of them dresses the two youngest children while the other mops the floor. The waking bell rings at 7:15, when the older children climb out of bed, dress, pray, and wash. Then the oldest daughter (age nine) rushes over to the next longhouse where she baby-sits for her aunt while the adults eat breakfast. Katie makes four feather beds, puts the baby on his toilet-training seat where he is watched by his eight-year-old sister, supervises the four-year-old as he dresses for kindergarten, bundles up the two-year-old, and just before the breakfast bell rings at 7:30, starts through the snow with her husband. The two-year-old is left with his grandfather, the preacher, who eats breakfast at home and therefore can watch the prekindergarten toddlers. Immediately after breakfast dishes, either the mother or the father gathers food to take back to feed the house children. Katie helps wash the dishes and then starts back to her house, picking up the two-year-old on the way. The moment she steps inside the door, the baby sitter, her second oldest daughter, rushes off to her breakfast and the mother proceeds to feed the house children. She will not see the kindergarten child until midafternoon; she will not see the school children for more than a moment until after the adults' supper dishes are washed at about 6:30. If her husband is working nearby or working alone, he may return for a snack about 9:00; otherwise he has a snack with the men at his place of work, or in the kitchen. Katie washes the dishes from the house children's breakfast and sews until 10:00. Then she takes her pail and goes to the kitchen to get food for the house children. The two-year-old is fed as soon as she returns, the nursing baby not until 11:00. At 11:15 the two-year-old takes a nap, and the baby is nursed and put into his crib. At 11:45 the adults eat; then the women wash the dishes and return to their houses where they can rest if the house children are sleeping. After resting they have a snack or sew until their husbands come for a snack at about 2:00. Katie sews until the kindergarten children return home about 3:30. She washes them and combs the front of her hair, and at 4:00 takes her pail and goes to the kitchen to get supper for the house children and the kindergartener. She feeds them, washes their dishes, and puts the baby in his crib for a nap. At 5:00 or 6:00 the community gathers for church. School-age children who are babysitters are excused from church to watch the pre-school and kindergarten children during church and the adults' supper. In a large colony there are two sitters assigned to each family so that each girl can take turns sitting and attending church and will not have to miss church more than half the time. In some colonies only one sitter is assigned to a family and therefore never attends church. After supper the school children must memorize their German school verses, while the little children play. Between 8:00 and 9:00 the children are given a snack, washed, their prayers supervised, and they are put to bed.

During the summer Katie has a great deal more work. Cleaning is much heavier in the summer because the children and adults track in dirt and mud; in the winter shoes are removed at the door and so the floors stay clean. There is also a great deal more colony work to do. It is an unusual weekday in the summer when the women have no colony work.

CHURCH SERVICE AND COMMUNITY INTEGRATION

The day's work in a Hutterite colony is suspended toward evening when all the adults and school children follow the preacher to the school house for the evening church service. The room is large, undecorated, and almost empty except for the benches for the worshippers. Everyone knows exactly where to sit. The members of the council face the audience, with the two preachers directly behind the table. The congregation sits according to age and sex; the youngest in the front seats, the oldest on the back benches, the women sit to the right as they enter from the rear of the building, the men sit to the left. A period of quiet ushers the group into a sacred interval of time. One of the preachers draws his chair to the desk, and in a seated position announces the hymn. With his German hymnbook open, he intones the first line. The congregation repeats each line after him, singing in unison an embellished version of the tune. The voice of the minister alternates with the loud, clear, penetrating song of the congregation. After three or four verses have been sung the leader sits back and the other preacher stands behind the desk. In a quiet, slow, monotone the second man beckons the listeners to hear the word of God, and the seventeenth-century interpretation of the text is read in a stylized sermon cadence.

The sermon is centered on a passage in Rom. 8:1–6. It exhorts the reader to "walk not after the flesh, but after the spirit. For to be carnally minded is death; but to be spiritually minded is life and peace." Emphasis is on "law and order" throughout the sermon. "Since God is a God of order, He demands that order should prevail and control us in every way, so that we may be conformed to His image." The sermon states that under the rule of Moses the people of God had to obey hundreds of laws, but Christ narrowed the rules down to two: "Thou shalt love the Lord thy God, and thy neighbor as thyself. This is no law for a Christian, since he can meet this requirement without compulsion. Practicing love will do away with all enforced laws. Love works no ill to his neighbor." The sermon ends with an extraordinary descending inflection. The exhortation to prayer is given and all kneel in a forward position with faces uplifted and hands folded at shoulder height. The preacher kneels on a small stool and audibly leads a long memorized prayer which lauds the righteous acts of God the Father; he pleads for patience, endurance, and faith to withstand the trials of the earthly life. There are two more verses of the hymn and a short benediction that commends the church to God. Thirty minutes have passed since the service began. The worshippers quickly proceed to the communal kitchen.

The Hutterite church service highlights some of the characteristics of their life pattern. *First,* there is no church building. The specific place where the worship service is held is unimportant. Sacred space is not confined to one room or one building, but encompasses all the central living space in the colony; it encompasses that area where God's order is respected. Many colonies worship in the school building, some in the dining hall, others in a different room in the kitchen complex. The only requirements are that the room be large, orderly, clean and unornamented, and that there be enough seats to assign everyone his place. *Second,* the church service contrasts with and supports their daily life. Special clothes are worn to special services, and only clean, neat clothes with long sleeves may be worn to church. Women, who seldom raise their voices when men are present, sing the hymns loudly and lustily, almost drowning out the men's voices. The tempo of the service is restful and unhurried: the hymns are sung slowly, the minister reads the sermon in a stylized chant and the prayer is long and recited softly. There is no hurry to be finished. The community symbolically returns to the time of its origins (to Jacob Hutter, to the twelve Apostles, and to the spiritual source of its power) so that it may re-create its existence beyond secular time.

Third, the church service emphasizes the importance of right order both in the seating of the members and in the sequence of the service. *Fourth,* the church service makes visible the authority pattern of the community and emphasizes its supernatural rightness. The women's seating is arranged by age, separate from the men. (Families do not sit together.) In the congregation men sit according to age, but on the council bench at the front of the room they sit by rank. On leaving the service the oldest man in the rear of the congregation leads. The oldest woman follows the youngest boy, and finally the council files out behind the youngest girl. The first minister leaves last, shepherding his flock. Everyone has an assigned place in church, a place that is determined by his position in the hierarchy of the colony. If anyone is absent her place is left empty and the community is incomplete. Each knows that his absence is noted and that he is missed. Thus, the church service corroborates the hierarchical structure of the colony, and reaffirms each individual in his or her God-given place in church, in the colony, and in the universe. Only he can fill his place; he is an intrinsic part of the larger whole.

Fifth, the church service not only serves a ritual function but also a didactic one. During this period the members are instructed in their discipline, their faith, their history, and the reason for their existence. *Sixth,* the church service is followed immediately by a community meal, by breaking bread together. Temporal bread immediately follows spiritual sustenance.

The church service reinforces the basic pattern of Hutterite life and simultaneously gives relief and depth by setting the sacred against the secular and thus permitting behavior and responses on a different plane. Within the service—protected, surrounded by, and observed by every other colony member—life becomes predictable, time is no longer fleeting, each individual is essential, and women may raise their voices in singing above those of the men. The words of the sermon are believed to flow from God and to remain part of God. Their message teaches anew and reinforces the values the full members have internalized. The church gathering is the highest moment of integration in the life of the community; it encompasses and gives meaning to all of life.

3 / Technology and Economic Patterns

Material property or "created things" are believed by the Hutterites to be gifts of God for the well-being of humankind. Because property is God-given, it must be communally owned and corporately shared. Private ownership of property "draws mankind away from spirituality and Godliness" (Rideman 1950:89) into carnality and greed. Since everyone is born with the natural human tendency to accumulate and own property, Hutterites believe that this tendency must be overcome with the help of God and the community. In this chapter we will describe how the informal behavior patterns function in relationship to the formal goals. Our observations are based on the three colonies in our sample, one from each of the three *Leut: Schmied-Leut, Darius-Leut,* and *Lehrer-Leut.* For purposes of identification, we will call the three sample colonies *Schmiedehof, Dariushof,* and *Lehrerhof.*

PRODUCTION AND RESOURCES

Most Hutterite colonies are dependent upon agricultural lands for their basic resources. *Dariushof* in Alberta was formed with a colony population of forty-nine persons. A former ranch of approximately 4,000 acres was acquired by lease agreement with an option to buy. Because the ranch had been a liability to its absentee owner and a "headache" to manage with hired labor, the colony took advantage of the opportunity to secure the location and branch earlier than is normally done. Only a fraction of the land was under cultivation at that time. Annual rainfall ranges from fourteen to seventeen inches, and droughts occur occasionally. The vegetation consists of grasslands and bluffs of silver leaf bush where moisture conditions are more favorable. Soils range from black to brown to sandy loam, and usually are well-supplied with nitrogen and organic matter but deficient in phosphorus. With good management, rotation of crops, and use of fertilizers, arable lands produce modest-to-good grain yields. Nonarable land is good pasture. The terrain is rolling, varying from moderate hills to sloughs and water holes. The colonists say "It is good cattle and grain country. If the loam can grow poplars and red willows, it can also produce grain." Gophers, beavers, muskrats, bobcats, lynx, coyotes, badgers, and deer interfere with the colony's productive enterprises. The gophers eat the planted grain and its roots, and the coyotes disturb the sheep. Cattle are in danger of falling into the holes made by badgers and muskrats, and cropland is flooded by beavers.

During each of the first few years the colony cleared from two to three hundred acres of bush land. Clearing, a seasonal activity, is an added burden for a small colony. In winter, when the ground is frozen, a tractor with a dozer is used to break off the small growth. The bush is heaped into windrows and left to dry for a year, and then is burned. Breaking the soil is done with a large, two-ton, colony-made plow. It takes three years to convert a parcel of virgin land to crop land.

The previously existing buildings on the ranch were adapted to the colony's pattern and function. The older buildings included a dairy barn, two hog barns, several grain bins, a horse barn, chicken barn, a repair shop, and two small dwelling units. The colony erected two longhouses and a communal kitchen. An abandoned schoolhouse was moved onto the colony site, and a kindergarten building and a seed-cleaning plant were moved in from the parent colony. Additional buildings erected included a root cellar, a smoke house, a shoe shop, a storage building with refrigeration unit, and additional buildings for poultry. With the parent colony less than fifteen miles away, it was possible for the new colony to begin with a modest amount of livestock, along with the use of machinery, services, and a loan from the parent colony. The annual cash intake after four years was slightly more than the expenditures. While the greatest returns were realized from the sale of grain and cattle, other diversified enterprises contributing to the cash income included sheep and wool, dairy products, ducks, geese, eggs, chickens, hogs, honey, and garden produce. The colony's largest trading center is one hundred miles away.

The six neighbors (twenty-four persons) are all within a six-mile radius of the colony. They are small farmers owning or operating from a quarter- to a half-section of land (320 acres). The colony has been willing to assist neighbors who have limited machinery and manpower to get their crops planted and harvested. County officials have generally been gratified with the positive influence of the colony. The amount of cattle thievery is believed to have declined, and the presence of the colony has resulted in added stability for the area. The colony leaders have expressed the view that the solution to the anti-Hutterite sentiment in Alberta is to locate new colonies in the north. Colony members are pleased with the present location.

The small number of people and the rather atypical beginning of the colony described above contrasts sharply with *Lehrerhof,* a somewhat older colony with a population of ninety persons. This Montana colony farms 16,000 acres of land. Only 4,500 acres are arable, and since summer fallowing is practiced, only 2,200 acres can be seeded each year. The remaining acres are grazing land and hay fields. The colony will often rent additional acreage from absentee farm owners when available. The soil is light, sandy, and shallow, and reputed to be "15–20-bushel land," in contrast to "50-bushel" lands in other nearby colonies. The elevation is 3,800 feet, the annual rainfall is 11 inches, and the mean annual snowfall is 33 inches. The colony, established in 1949, is located on the eastern slope of the Rocky Mountain terrain and is within the Chinook wind belt, which has a marked effect on the area's climate. Wind erosion is a serious problem, making strip farming essential.

Crops harvested in a recent year at *Lehrerhof* were 28,000 bushels of barley, 12,000 bushels of wheat, and 9,000 bushels of oats. The hay crop amounted to 36,000 bales, which were stored for winter feeding. Wheat is sold for cash during the fall and winter, and all other grains are consumed by the colony livestock. The colony's acreage allotment is limited to about 700 acres of wheat. 900 acres of barley, and 600 acres of oats, If a full crop is harvested, no subsidy is paid, but if the

Harvesting potatoes. Large machines and new equipment are characteristic of agricultural colonies.

crops are hailed out or yield poorly, the colony is eligible for a subsidy. All crops, including several hundred acres of alfalfa hay, are sprayed for weeds by a colony-made, self-propelled sprayer. If allowed to grow, weeds absorb the little available moisture there is for plant life.

There are 500 head of cattle on *Lehrerhof,* and 200 are fed during the winter. A dairy herd of thirty cows provides products for colony consumption but the cream is marketed. Five teams of horses and five saddle horses are maintained for working with range cattle and for hauling supplies during the severe winter months. The several thousand ducks that are consumed entirely by the colony are fattened during the summer. Several thousand geese, most of which are marketed in nearby towns, are raised and processed each year. Hog production is organized on a continuous basis. One barn contains the brood sows and their young, and another is used for fattening the hogs. Barns are equipped with running water, a chain drag to carry out the manure, a system of ventilation, water heaters, and a heating unit with infrared lamps to keep the young pigs warm. The colony raises about 1,000 lambs each year, and sheep are a good source of income from the wool and lambs sold. Mutton is also an important source of meat for colony consumption. Sheep raising provides work for the young men on the colony during two annual periods when other work is minimal. Lambing takes place during February, March, and April, when the sheep require almost constant care.

Lehrerhof moved from a parent colony in Canada and was the ninth to locate in Montana. The present site was chosen with the aid of real-estate agents, who showed colony representatives five possible locations. The advantage of the Montana site was its proximity to a good road and reasonable distance (sixty-five miles) from a large trading center. Several disadvantages of the present site have become apparent to the members. The major complaint of the colony is that the land is too poor and the rainfall too limited to produce enough crops. Several informants expressed the view that the colony should have moved to Saskatchewan, but when the group voted to go to Montana, most members argued: "If other colonies can succeed in Montana, we can too."

When it was formed, *Lehrerhof* was considered modern because it acquired trucks and electricity at that time. In comparison with its own daughter colony, however, formed after twelve years, it was "old-fashioned." In 1964 the householder said, "We work with outdated facilities, and if we had the capital we would install a modern dairy with a milking parlor, a modern poultry barn, a new hog barn, gas heating in the homes, make a large kitchen, and buy better tractors." Since capital was lacking for such improvements and the present facilities were adequate to get by, improvements were modest. However, thirty years later all these goals had been achieved.

The resource pattern of *Schmiedehof*, a third colony, has many of the agricultural characteristics of the two discussed above, but is distinguished by a greater degree of mechanization. Its population numbers 124 persons. Its soil is more productive than the two colonies described, and its acreage is the least of the three colonies, or approximately 5,000 acres. The productive enterprises of turkey raising, egg production, and hog production are augmented by a larger labor force as well as more modern equipment. Large chicken barns housing up to 10,000 laying hens each are automated with feeding, egg gathering, egg grading, and ventilation equipment.

This poultry barn houses 20,000 laying hens and is managed by one young man.

Mechanization appears to be more characteristic of the newly formed colonies, provided the land is productive. Investments in machinery are allocated to the newly formed colony as a rule, and newer types of machinery are acquired in preference to older and less efficient models. New colonies generally have a limited supply of labor and need labor-saving equipment.

The householder of a colony, functioning as the secretary-treasurer of the corporation, makes a yearly report to members. This report is prepared by a certified accountant and often with the aid of legal counsel. The colonies pay municipal or local taxes and school taxes as well as state and federal taxes. In Canada and in the United States the colonies are taxed on their corporate earnings. Should a colony have a "poor year," whether by hail, drought, or poor management, there will be very little cash available for improvements, clothing, or extras. For example, purchase of yard goods will be held at a minimum, and although new black denim must be bought for the men's work trousers, the women will be given less cloth and they may not get a new dress that year.

The various enterprises are carefully considered by the colony at the yearly meeting. Whether to expand, mechanize, or diminish one enterprise, such as hog or turkey raising, will be important for the welfare of the whole colony. Important factors entering into decision making for the productive enterprises are: the cleavage between the old and young men, since the younger are more prone to support mechanization; the ability of the person in charge of a given enterprise; and the ability of the group to arrive at an amicable consensus. Since consensus is more important for "the good of the colony" than sheer efficiency, the Hutterites have refrained generally from speculative production. A large volume with a small but steady profit is

Grain storage facilities on a Hutterite colony.

often considered more important than enterprises yielding the largest margin of profit. Their productive strategy of maintaining a wide diversity of agricultural practices so there will be work for everyone throughout the year has been hampered in Canada by the quota system, which penalizes them for "overproduction."

The Hutterites recognize that to be economically competitive they must adopt the best available technology. They have in many cases accepted more innovations than their neighbors and are often more progressive in outlook. They see no inconsistency in using modern, twentieth-century machines to preserve their sixteenth-century religious and social institutions (Ryan 1977: 274). What puts them ahead, says John Bennett (1967: 275), is not only their favorable attitude toward innovation but their sheer scale of operations. The availability of farm labor and good credit at the banks helps to assure their economic capability. Better machines help to preserve rather than erode their values.

The Hutterites produce large amounts of agricultural commodities in the states and provinces where they live. Ryan (1977: 152–205) reported that in Manitoba they produced 31 percent of all hogs in that province, 17 percent of all laying hens, 20 percent of turkeys, 62 percent of ducks, and 95 percent of Manitoba's geese. The Hutterite productive capacity has helped them to support their steadily growing population. Large families have been the norm among Hutterites in North America.

WORK

The Hutterite colony is a community of work. All persons are required to work according to their ability, and the professed purpose of labor is that the needs of all may be supplied. The productive capacity of a colony varies with the size of its population, acreage, and the number of adults in the labor force. In a colony of about average population size such as *Lehrerhof,* there are 101 persons: 48 men and 53 women. The labor force (persons aged fifteen or over) consists of 24 males and 24 females; half of these 48 persons are married couples. Generally speaking, a colony with the greatest number of workers has the greatest productive capacity. All major decisions, whether they pertain to discipline or economic activity, are made by the *Gemein* and are implemented by the council. The same group makes policy for both economic and religious matters. Typically, the preacher's influence overshadows the economic policy of the colony. He is always the president of the colony corporation. The second preacher serves as his assistant.

Normally, on Sunday evening after supper the householder comes to the preacher's house with a summary of the work that needs to be done during the coming week. Together they formulate a plan and make assignments. Specific orders are given daily for jobs that are not routine. Two of the unmarried men are assigned to each of the large diesel tractors used for major field work. They are given the job title of "engineers" and work in shifts during the height of the field work. The older of the two persons on each tractor is "boss" and is responsible for keeping the machine serviced, overhauled, and repaired. A tractor operator has a close relationship with the shop mechanic. The combines are assigned to married men. During harvest or haying, work loads are rearranged for maximum efficiency. The cattle man, the German teacher, and the shop mechanic join the harvesting crew. Older persons, including the preacher, drive trucks or help wherever work is needed. If a tractor or combine breaks down, the shop mechanic helps the operator to get it repaired. If the two cannot repair it, the operator informs the householder, who may refer the problem to the council if major costs or a trip to town are necessary. However, during rush seasons the normal steps of acquiring approval in the case of a major breakdown need not apply. A mechanic may initiate expenditures for repairs in the interests of efficiency.

The amount and type of work reveals a dynamic pattern integrated with the seasons. The leadership strives to provide enough work for all males during the entire year. Lack of work could mean the breakdown of a smooth-running colony. In summer there is a greater need for labor than in winter. During the winter months the colony absorbs the additional labor by reassigning jobs and by giving each department additional younger apprentices. Most males have two jobs in which they have achieved some specialization. The gardener becomes a carpenter in winter. The preacher, who looks after the geese in summer, concentrates on book binding in winter. The pigman has an extra boy assigned to him. The carpenter has two extra helpers in winter making household furniture, and the shop mechanic has additional help for overhauling machinery.

The constant need for improving and expanding facilities absorbs much of the off-season labor. A newly formed colony with a small kitchen must build a larger complex as its population expands. Additional buildings must also be planned. During slack work periods the colony may remodel or build. The task begins with the search for a supply of lumber. Often obsolete buildings are secured from a neighbor.

This colony prepares feed supplements for other colonies and for the market.

The building is dismantled carefully by colony labor and is transported. Bulldozing underbrush when the ground is frozen is a part of the work activity of one colony in winter. In a Manitoba colony, chasing foxes with a snowmobile and hounds is part of the winter work schedule. "Unless we get about twenty foxes each winter, we will have trouble with the geese in summer," said the preacher.

In work and productive activity, competition and experimentation are desired and encouraged. Making the soil more productive, even to the extent of maintaining experimental plots, and improving farm machines are encouraged. The competition between department managers proves to be healthy for the welfare of the colony. It does not involve direct competition between individuals or their assigned status but between income-producing phases of the operations. The foreman of the chickens may accumulate a great deal of knowledge about the best methods of building, ventilating, feeding, processing, and the cost of producing a case of eggs. The dairyman learns all he can from farm magazines, agricultural experimentation publications, neighbors, and salesmen about livestock and the prevention of disease. Selective borrowing from the outside is common, and inventions in one colony will diffuse to others, often in a very short time.

The work tempo varies also with the seasons. In winter the pressure to complete any particular job is not as great as in summer, when in many colonies the growing season is relatively short. Work is not done in an erratic manner; the work pattern is predictable, regular, and satisfying. There is little effort to make work last. In reality,

The electronic controls for this feed mill were built by the Hutterite operator of the plant.

there is often some leisure time and a minimum of physical exertion. Many work assignments are completed before the end of the day. When this happens, men tend to gather in the central shop. By gravitating to unfinished tasks before the end of the day, the individual is in effect showing readiness to assist in unassigned tasks. Boys will run errands and older men will participate on a voluntary basis. The equalization of work is achieved by assignment and modified by the need for social participation after the work is done in tasks that are unstructured.

One fall day the colony decided to build a much-needed goose corral to protect the fowl from coyotes. The informal discussions about the procedures for building were very noisy, but there was no ill will or friction between disagreeing persons. After the major decisions were made the householder said of the preacher, who was also the oldest person in the colony, "Pete knows best—he's the oldest and knows the most."

Boards were utilized from a distant pile of lumber in a preferred order. The persons nailing the boards took them from a nearby pile and not from the person who carried them to the scene. Respect for the older persons, as evidenced by refusal to hurry them, slowed down efficiency. Males of all ages were present, and even three-year-old children were imitating the older ones. Six-year-old boys hammered nails into the siding with hammers. Their obstruction of the work of older persons was not resented; they were not told to get out of the way, nor were they told how to use the

Some colonies make and repair shoes, saddles and harness.

tools. During the afternoon several of the older men were called away from the scene to the colony's shop and the equipment was not put away. That night it rained, and the next morning the householder was very unhappy about the tools that had rusted due to the precipitation.

Persons are very conscious of rank. Any attempt to change a person's status is met with rebuke from one's peers. The result is a cautious, humble attitude in group situations. A person who suggests a course of action must be prepared to retract his statements. Opinions are often presented passively as if they were those of another person. One obvious advantage is that a great many proposals can be considered and the one that appeals to the majority will be adopted. The disadvantage of strong authority patterns are certain kinds of functional inefficiencies. One tractor operator, for example, did not repair his machine until it broke down because he had no authority to start repairing until it did actually break down. A younger person will not suggest to an older person that his movements are too slow, or that his talking with a stranger is slowing down the work. A young man may be afraid to propose solutions for fear of usurping authority from his older superior. A child will be punished for disobeying orders but not for breaking a dish.

At a council meeting concerned with buying a tractor, an individual who likes a particular model will present his case without appealing to personal references. He may present general ideas or the experiences of neighbors and equipment dealers. Any member may modify the proposal. No individual may claim sole credit for an idea; the group as a whole assumes authorship. This process allows all persons to share in decision making and to identify with the end product. Even though the individual may not engage personally in the decision making, he enjoys situations that involve group decision making.

EXPANSION AND BRANCHING

All Hutterite colonies are basically alike in their social organization and expansion characteristics. Each colony forms its own new colony by a planned method of splitting. A parent colony deliberately plans a new daughter colony in advance. This process of "branching out," as Hutterites call it, is made necessary by population growth and requires delicate management of capital assets; investments; redistribution of colony authority, family, and kinship factors; and work patterns. When a colony reaches a maximal population size (130–150 persons), Hutterites begin to sense management problems–problems of affluence, of inefficiency, and of supervision. The growth span between branchings varies, but the average is about fourteen years. During this time a colony may increase from about 70 to 130 persons.

The growth span of a colony is marked by successive stages from the time it is formed until it forms a daughter colony. The new colony must work hard to pay off 50 percent of its debts; the parent colony is usually responsible for the other half of the debts. A debt-free colony will expand its land holdings and obtain more equipment to provide more jobs for its growing population. A third stage is the period of affluence when a colony is able to save money for expansion, to loan money to other needy colonies, and to make and install many labor-saving devices. Each of these stages has distinct capital, management, and labor problems.

In order to establish a new colony, the existing colony must save or borrow sufficient capital. A rule of thumb requires that a colony must accumulate at least one million dollars. This amount is needed for the initial investment of land and equipment. A new communal kitchen may cost up to one-half million dollars. Most colonies must save over a period of about fifteen years. Some will branch out after twelve years. Poor colonies borrow money from the well-to-do colonies. The decision to branch out is not only an economic proposition but is dependent upon the ease of obtaining land, the population pressure, and how well the "politics" of the colony are managed. Most colonies will form a legal corporation in keeping with the laws of the state or province in which they are located. Some will incorporate when achieving a debt-free status; others will form a separate corporation at the time of branching and agree to share equally the debts for the new colony. As a minimum requirement, a colony needs about sixty persons for branching. By contrasting the new, small colony with the large colony, the different needs and solutions to communal living can be compared. Each new colony is formed in such a manner that comparable age and sex distributions of the population are maintained. In the small colony of approximately sixty persons, about half are under the age of fifteen. Of the remaining adults, about fifteen are males who carry on the major work and managerial responsibility. The minimum positions in a new colony include preacher (who may temporarily serve also as householder), field manager, cattle man, school teacher, and council member at large. Five of the fifteen men are normally twenty-five or older, and only they are eligible to occupy foreman positions since they are married. The remaining ten men may be unmarried and most of them are unbaptized; their work is supervised. A number of positions are combined and held by a single foreman until younger men become eligible. Thus the colony is characterized by much work, many potential jobs and status positions, and a minimum of struggle for the more important roles.

Both men and women tend to be overworked in a new colony. The shop mechanic has more work than he can do himself. He needs younger men who show aptitude for a number of skills like electrical work and welding. Depending on the size of the cattle herd, two men may be necessary. During the seeding and harvest seasons, great demands are made on the entire colony. At least four or five combines are necessary to harvest the crop in the short time before winter sets in. The combines are operated, when weather permits, on a twenty-four-hour basis. Several truck drivers are required to haul the grain. Others are required to swathe, and the mechanic is often busy with emergency repair work. Fuel is transported to the fields, and in case of a breakdown a mobile welding unit is brought into the fields.

New colonies may be formed within a few miles of existing colonies or as far away as five hundred miles. About thirty miles is considered to be a good distance.

New colonies seldom start with the maximum number of acres desired. They may acquire from 3,000 to 4,000 acres and increase the acreage as opportunity and need arises. More land is secured, preferably adjoining the colony property, but other nearby lands are also purchased both to increase their acreage and to obtain quotas.

Quota restrictions, as well as land limitations, intensify internal problems, particularly in a bulging colony where there is competition for roles and a need to expand the work program.

After a colony has reached maturity, the ratio of qualified persons to available positions is reversed. There are about thirty-five males over the age of fifteen in the mature colony. About sixteen men who are over the age of thirty hold all the important roles and status positions. Another five persons are between the ages of twenty-five and thirty and expect to be assigned to important positions soon. But since all appointments tend to be permanent, the opportunities for younger married men are limited. Thus, the upward mobility that normally comes with age is thwarted by the scarcity of positions. Due partly to the quota system and partly to the general trend towards specialization, there are a diminished number of leadership positions, which further contributes towards internal pressure and is contributing to smaller colony size. With a larger labor force and greater specialization, the division of labor has become more specific, overlapping jobs are eliminated, and competitive activity tends to develop along family lines. The fathers who hold important positions of power have a slight advantage in getting their sons into the favored jobs. Thus, competition reaches a stage that is no longer conducive to economic productivity but to social unrest. Work rules are more difficult to enforce where the division of labor is refined and very specific. In a young colony there is a decisive age difference between the leaders and the followers, while in a mature colony the age differences tend to disappear among people who are eligible for the important jobs and the rules are harder to maintain. Factionalization and formation of cliques signal the need for branching. In branching, disruptive tendencies are mitigated, and competition is channeled into expansion.

Following the decision to branch, several years may be required to form the new colony. A suitable site must be agreed upon by the whole colony, often with very limited opportunities available to them. A preferred site has the following features: availability of a good water supply and, if possible, nearness to a lake or creek; good soil and, if possible, a history of productivity; rainfall; adequate growing season; drainage; and a distinct distance from towns but access to roads and to markets. Potential fire hazards and hailstorms also must be considered. Dwellings are preferably on an elevation higher than the rest of the grounds and, insofar as it is possible, near the center of the acreage. An equitable amount of space between living houses, the communal kitchen, the school house, and kindergarten are important to the women. The women are permitted to view the prospective new location and to express preferences. After the land is secured, it may be farmed and dwellings may be built over an intervening period. As a colony grows, more buildings are added to an overall layout that can accommodate additional buildings. Frequently, the colony buildings are also hedged in with trees and shrubs that are needed for protection against the wind and unwanted annoyances. Although branching practices differ slightly among the three *Leut,* the ideals of impartiality are the same. The following branching procedures in a *Lehrer-Leut* colony illustrates the process.

Moving day had been set for Thursday, and many trucks from the nearest colonies (as far as three hundred miles) had come to help. The day before moving day, all members packed their belongings. Since no one knew who was going to move, all had to be prepared, even though half of the families would have to remain.

The cattle were divided into two herds and a lot was drawn to determine which would be moved. The lot system was also used to divide certain kinds of small equipment. It had been agreed that the new colony would purchase additional new equipment and new tractors. The mother colony provided the capital for branching, and the two colonies decided to remain a single corporation until the debts were liquidated. By precedent, the "mother" colony was to retain the older machinery. The milking equipment was not to be removed and the new colony would obtain its own new equipment as capital assets permitted. Benches and desks were removed from the school, since the group staying did not have need for all of this furniture.

The preacher, with the aid of his assistant, listed families on the blackboard in two groups, each of which was headed by the name of one of the preachers. Family heads were permitted to choose between the two preachers. Older people were grouped according to their known preferences, but a balance between the two groups was worked out that took into account age, sex, family size, and relatedness. On Wednesday afternoon, all the baptized men gathered in the school to consider the plan of their leaders. The women anxiously waited at home to hear the outcome. After the evening meal, the lot was drawn between the two preachers to see which of the two groups would move. The older preacher drew the first slip of paper from the hat. It indicated he was to remain. On Thursday morning the loaded trucks rolled away with the assistant preacher and his group. Those on the colony quietly unpacked their belongings, sad to be separated from friends and family, but happy that they were allowed to remain in familiar surroundings.

Lehrer-Leut rules require that a colony must have the consent of all other colonies within the *Leut* to form a new colony. This is not only a formal courtesy but a check on the success and reputation of the communal system as a whole. Successful communal living depends upon the well-being of every newly formed colony. If a new colony would run into difficulty with crop failure or suffer financial reverses, every colony would be obligated to come to its aid. Among the *Darius-Leut,* a colony may branch without formal consent of the others, and their practices permit one of two factions in a colony to "volunteer" to move to the new location. But this "volunteering," some say, works against impartiality since it is usually a kinship group that does the volunteering. If a colony should branch without the consent of others and experiences financial reverses, it will have difficulty borrowing money from other colonies. Population growth is not the only "push" factor in branching. If the colony is divided into two factions, if the preachers, or the preacher and the householder do not get along too well, colonies will branch years before their numbers are considered sufficiently large. Branching tends to resolve characteristic conflicts between brother sibships.

Branching is supported by strong authority patterns. Only the will of God is strong enough to separate family members, parents from older children, brothers from each other, and to break personal, sentimental ties. Individual desires must be subordinated to the will of the community, through which the will of God is always manifested. If the level of spiritual dedication is high, branching can be achieved with a minimum of problems; if low, then long-standing grievances can result. The highest ideal to be achieved in branching is impartiality involving persons and property.

CONSUMPTION

"Need" and "equality" are two professed principles that govern the sharing of goods in the Hutterite colony. "Fellowship in holy things" requires sharing of temporal goods; "one person must not have abundance and another suffer want, but there must be equality" (Rideman 1950:88). Life in this world is a means to attain the goal of salvation after death. The physical existence of human life must be controlled in such a way that the divine pattern is reflected during life. The carnal appetite for food and drink, for example, must be controlled by the spiritual nature and kept in moderation. The carnal nature is believed to express itself in the adornment of the body, and in pleasures that cater to the "lusts of the eye," such as makeup, movies, television shows, dancing, and worldly music. Since these things must be avoided, they are not "needs" and not part of the consumption pattern.

The major expenses (see accompanying table) for underwriting the productive phases of a colony are these: the purchase of land, equipment, fertilizer, building supplies, fuel, seed, feed, lumber, livestock, veterinary costs, utilities, and insurance. The modernization of equipment or repair of existing farm equipment is a major expense. Most colonies make weekly trips to nearby towns or cities. Specific members, with the consent of the preacher or council, frequently go on long trips of several hundred miles, to attend weddings, funerals, and to purchase bees, livestock, and supplies. Travel equipment, which includes vans and large trucks, is important to them.

In the table, the $706 paid out for fines includes fines for traffic violations in town and the failure of Hutterites to obtain special permits for transporting large equipment on highways. The willingness to pay such fines expresses a conflict of colony time patterns versus worldly time patterns. When the colony "boss" goes to town, often accompanied by several men and women who have appointments, he operates according to colony time patterns and not according to conceptions of privately owned time.

The average income over expenditures for forty-three colonies in Manitoba showed a profit of $32,000 (Ryan 1977:235). By 1995 profits from marketing turkeys and hogs pushed the new income much higher. In South Dakota the new profit of colonies ranged from one million to six million dollars.

Hutterites are able to offset some of the high costs of large-scale farming by adapting machines to their regional needs and by doing their own repair work. Massive tractors and large trucks are repaired and maintained by colony repair shops. The labor force is trained by practical experience and by limited exposure to machine shops outside the colony. Occasionally, men will take a short course in wiring or welding in a technical school outside the colony. The shop absorbs labor when idleness would be a danger to the social cohesion of the colony, thus keeping the system efficient at minimum cost. These shops utilize scrap iron and steel, often available from city dumps at a nominal cost.

The shop provides an inexpensive way to mechanize operations. New equipment may be used for several years, then repainted, reconditioned and sold, or used equipment may be bought, and skilled Hutterite mechanics may improve and adapt it to colony needs. This applies to modernizing hog and poultry barns, including the installation of feeding and egg-gathering equipment. Hutterites often improve the existing models of farm machinery or adapt them to their purposes. One mechanic

ANNUAL EXPENSES FOR A DIVERSIFIED AGRICULTURAL COLONY, 1991

Land payment and taxes	$325,138
Farm machinery	256,070
Fertilizer and chemicals	251,660
Repair, hardware, and electrical supplies	247,429
Fuel	155,533
Feed	101,299
Market board, poultry eggs	72,287
Seed	67,602
Lumber	67,080
Groceries	46,393
Dry goods and shoes	31,569
Electricity	28,525
Natural gas	28,230
Livestock	23,526
Insurance	20,117
General sales tax (GST)	20,117
Physicians, medicine, and medical plan	17,535
Veterinary	11,799
Legal fees	7,138
Travel	7,023
Telephone	4,118
Books and stamps	1,838
Fines	706
TOTAL	$1,792,732

constructed cabs of plexiglass for the grain combines long before farm implement companies sold them on the market. Another made an attachment to a combine that prevented the stones from entering the cylinder, thus protecting the machine from considerable damage. Cultivators adapted to dry-land farming are made by colonies in Canada. Specialized machines such as hydraulic rockpickers and tractor cabs are manufactured by colony shops. The Noble Blade, widely used by Canadian colonies, acts like a gigantic knife slicing the soil at a depth of about five inches. This method of cultivation, an alternative to disc plowing, reduces wind erosion. A capping knife for extracting honey from honeycombs was made by a colonist and was later patented and produced by an outside firm. Disputes over patent rights became a problem among the *Schmied-Leut* in the late 1980s.

The taboos that are so strong against individual ownership do not apply to the economic gains for the colony as a corporate body. There are limited occasions when a colony will not take subsidies or refunds from the government. Some colonies refused compensation for missile sites and underground cables on their property. As a pacifist Christian group, their policy in this instance was not to interfere with the government and at the same time not accept payment for damages or for right of way.

Attitudes toward money stress saving rather than spending, and accumulating it where possible. The colony's ability to acquire goods at minimal costs and to market products at maximum prices encompasses a wide scope of activity. A few examples of thrift and careful management are these:

Several Canadian colonies pool their orders for watermelons from a Texas dealer each year. Single colonies will take 3,000 pounds and pay from one to one-and-a-half cents per pound. Baby foxes were captured and reared until they were old enough to collect bounty. Large petroleum tanks discarded by the oil company were converted into grain storage bins. Damaged canned goods were bought at reduced prices from chain stores. Grain that had been damaged by fire was purchased from elevators for half price and fed to the livestock. Used electric motors and generators were secured from discarded sources and rewound and repaired by the colony mechanics. A Montana colony drove its trailer-truck to South Carolina to obtain earth-moving equipment from Army surplus stock. Colony bosses frequently receive courtesies from stock dealers and salesmen who covet the business of the colony. Such favors might include free subscriptions to farm magazines that directly benefit the colony. One mechanic earned hourly wages for the colony by repairing upholstery on trucks for outsiders. Some colonies will help repair roads for the county or municipality.

DISTRIBUTION

"To each according to his needs" is the professed or formal pattern. "Each was given what he needed according to the measure" (Rideman 1950:88). "Needs" are defined by the colony system, and "equality" does not mean that all have the same needs, or that all receive the same amount and kind of food, furniture, or clothing. A significant aspect of the professed beliefs is that the carnal desire of the individual for property is considered so "strong" that the help of colony members is needed to live according to the divine pattern. The thorough distrust of individual motives built into the colony system is openly acknowledged: "In the fear of God we observe and watch one another . . . telling each his faults, warning, and rebuking with all diligence" (Rideman 1950:131–132). The Hutterite definition of need and equality varies from colony to colony, but the main features on the information level are illustrated here.

Food is served in two dining rooms, one for the adults and one for the children. The only adults who do not eat in the dining hall are the two preachers, who eat in the apartment of the head preacher. The precedent for this practice, Hutterites say, is that God-fearing people hold their ministers in high esteem, and that it allows the leaders the necessary privacy for counsel and the opportunity for others to bring needs and complaints to their attention. Each family apartment also has a kitchen corner for feeding preschool children and for serving snacks to visitors and at coffee time between meals.

The manner in which clothing is distributed is illustrative of the Hutterite concepts of need and equality. Clothing can be saved, modified, and exchanged. The head tailoress of each colony keeps a book which specifies the kinds and amount of clothing allocated to individuals and family heads. The colony book has been handed down through the years. Allotments and specifications are determined by the rules of each *Leut,* although many rules are obsolete or modified in some way. The tailoress keeps a record of the materials distributed to each family, and each mother usually keeps a record of what her family received. The yardage is distributed several times each year from the storeroom. A family is not necessarily obligated to use material for the purpose specified, and the material need not necessarily be used by the person for whom it was allocated. It can be traded between families, with other colonies, or given as gifts.

The following allotments to a newly married couple apply in *Lehrerhof*. A groom shall have from his colony: one bed with mattress and pillow, a table and two chairs, a closet, cupboard, stove, wall clock, sewing machine, and a set of Hutterite books. The bride's colony is to provide the following: 7 yards and 8 inches of bed-spread material, 10 yards of comforter cover, material for a mattress pad 60 inches wide, six pillow cases, 12 yards of material for a feather comforter, a kettle, enamel dish, one cup and saucer, spoon, knife, fork, soup pail, scissors, and a large chest. Bedding as well as clothing is homemade from yardgoods. The pillows and feather bedding are usually made by the bride's family before the wedding day. Feathers for making comforters were formerly allocated at the rate of sixteen pounds per person, but now a couple has the option to take a mattress and only twelve pounds of feathers. Eight pounds of feathers are allocated for each new baby. In many colonies dacron batting is given instead of feathers.

Beds and bedding are distributed according to the number of children: with the first child the family gets a crib, with the second a *Schlafbank* (a settee that opens into a bed for two children), with the fourth child a second *Schlafbank,* with the sixth child a second bed, with the eighth child a third bed, with the tenth child a third *Schlafbank,* and with the twelfth child a fourth bed. Today a bed is given instead of a *Schlafbank.*

Bedding for the first baby includes: a crib cover 1 by 1 yard, a mattress pad for the crib 41 by 24 inches, a pillow 22 by 19 inches, a flannel pad 22 by 19 inches, a larger pad 36 to 24 inches, and a crib sheet. For every baby, the family receives 2 yards for shirts, 4 yards for two little dresses, 2 yards for aprons, 2 yards of flannel for underwear, and 4 yards for diapers. Obviously, this is not enough for a year, but with the gifts from relatives the supply is ample. A mother may always draw upon her regular allotment of yardgoods for the family.

The rule book specifies to the inch how much yardage each person shall have on the basis of his age. Ten-year-old boys shall have material for a jacket annually at the rate of 3 yards and 6 inches. Eleven-year-old boys shall be allotted 3 yards and 12 inches, and men over fourteen shall receive 4 yards. When someone is over-weight, he shall have 9 additional inches. Clothing allotments change most dramati-cally when boys and girls become adults (fourteen years old in *Lehrerhof*). The rule book allows 9 yards of material for a girl's dress. It takes only about 5 yards to make a modern dress, but the traditional allotment is still passed out.

The amount and variety of yardgoods tends to become an object of bickering be-tween the male-female subcultures. The colonies buy from salesmen who frequent the colonies. The tailoress knows how much the colony needs and will inquire about the price and quality. The householder must give consent to the cost, and the preacher must consent to the colors. After a clothing salesman visited the colony, one preacher said: "The women have so much material, they don't know what to do. They are just like children who don't know what they should have and who don't re-alize what it costs." His wife, who was standing nearby, denied the charge. Women admit that the material is stronger than years ago, and the men say they cannot pos-sibly wear out everything in such a short time. Women do not hesitate to buy the less durable material so it will wear out quicker, thereby providing them with a new dress sooner. Some men and boys are finicky about colors and the fit of their shirts and trousers. Boys may refuse to wear shirts if they do not like the color.

Each household is assigned sleeping rooms according to the size of the family. A rule of thumb is one additional room for every four children. But should the colony have spare rooms, use is made of them. Frequently, brothers and sisters sleep in the same room until they are ten. The younger members of the family always sleep in the bedroom with their parents. However, as living apartments are getting larger with the incorporation of basements, and family size is decreasing, there are fewer people to a bedroom. One older Hutterite woman commented that it was more cozy when they were more crowded. Every family has a box in a root cellar for storing vegetables and fruits, and beverages allocated regularly to family heads. The amount of beer and wine allocated to each family varies with each colony. In one colony each person fourteen or over receives twelve bottles of beer quarterly. Wine is made by the colony from grapes and rhubarb, and each adult receives one quart per month. Beverages served at weddings and at butchering time are above the family allotment. Twelve bottles of soft drink are allocated to school children (under fourteen) quarterly. Persons over fourteen who prefer soft drinks to beer may obtain twice the number of bottles. When special treats are baked on Tuesdays, each person older than six months receives the same amount.

The distribution pattern reinforces the social hierarchy. It is characterized by strong authority patterns and by practices that are adaptive. Equality is established on the basis of age and sex. Socially sanctioned needs, not individual wants, are satisfied. Impartiality and sharing are emphasized by the formal beliefs. Abuses of the system do exist but what matters most to the colonists is not that there are abuses but that there is a right pattern from which exceptions can be granted. The important thing is that the pattern supports the sharing so that respect for the system is maintained.

ATTITUDES TOWARD PROPERTY AND RECIPROCITY

Personal property to an adult Hutterite is defined as: "Something given to me from the colony for me. Once it has been given, it is mine to use." The concept of property means the right to use but not to possess. Personal belongings include those items that are formally given to the individual by the colony, plus anything acquired by the individual with money from his small allowance. Belongings a person may have are kept in a chest under lock and key given to the individual. Personal belongings are passed on to the children and sometimes to other relatives before or after the individual dies. Yardgoods which have not been utilized for clothing are returned to the colony storehouse at the time of death. Ideally, all personal gifts from neighbors or outsiders are reported to the householder. In practice, individuals are permitted to keep some of these gifts that they may have earned in return for work or favors. Some of these gifts benefit the colony. In one colony several men had received as a gift a pair of binoculars. They were used by the sheepherder and cattle foreman in their work. There is little sentimental value attached to old clothing, dishes, or furniture. Unless there is a utilitarian value, antiques are not kept for sentimental reasons but are generally worn out. Although cross-stiched decorative handkerchiefs were made until recently by the girls for their boyfriends, the practice is dying out. The complaint is that it takes too long and it is easier to buy a gift in the store. Books are an exception to the general indifference to sentimental property. A book may be valued if it is old and if a relative has copied it. The sons of preachers who are elected as preachers have priority privileges for certain books, especially sermon books. Although having one's picture taken is technically taboo, having the photographs once the picture is taken carries little negative sanction.

For children growing up in a colony, there are two kinds of property: things under lock and key to which access is forbidden, and materials not locked up. The latter are accessible and available for use. The practice of using padlocks on the colony "is necessary to keep children from getting into everything." There is a widespread expectation that children will get into everything. One preacher said: "Opportunity makes thieves, and we have to keep things locked up." All the school girls at *Lehrerhof* from grade three to eight keep their chests locked "or else our brothers would take everything," they say. Each jealously carries her own key at all times to guard her little secret world containing chewing gum, perfume, coins, scarves, pictures, letters, and keepsakes. Boys in one colony cannot be trusted with slingshots, as windows are their favorite targets. In other colonies, slingshots are accepted play things. Young people form specific behavior patterns toward property in a colony. When they are old enough to go outside of the colony and on trips to town, they must learn a new set of attitudes and acquire the appropriate restraints against taking property that is not locked up. One householder who complained about the relaxed care of tools said: "Colony people seem to think that since things don't belong to them, they do not need to be careful. They are more careless than outsiders." Mentioned were shoes, pencils, and tools. "Our colony people forget that eventually the colony must pay for everything," he said. Attitudes toward property and the colony's ability to inculcate these values vary considerably from one colony to another.

Attitudes toward property are revealed by reciprocity patterns, that is, the rules that apply in the exchange of economic and social favors. These rules of exchange also reveal the pattern of social distance, within the colony and outside of it, and the attitude of the colonists toward themselves. A scheme for understanding these relationships (Sahlins 1965:145) would include three types of reciprocity: generalized reciprocity, balanced reciprocity, and negative reciprocity.

Generalized reciprocity is purely altruistic assistance without specific obligation to return the favor. Thus, in a colony, the young are nourished. The goods collectively produced are distributed on the domestic level to the individual. Individuals in the colony are the recipients of sharing and hospitality for an unspecified duration. They receive small monthly allowances for which they need not reciprocate or give an accounting to anyone. Traditionally, a small amount of spending money was given to those individuals who went to town with the colony officials who were conducting weekly business. Colonies now give a monthly allowance to every person in the colony whether they go to town or not. The allowance varies with the rules of each colony. In *Lehrerhof,* adult men receive one dollar per month and adult women receive one dollar every six months. In *Dariushof,* kindergartners receive five cents, school children ten cents, and all adults receive one dollar monthly.

Balanced reciprocity is direct exchange, a two-way flow of goods and favors. Gifts or favors given require that the equivalent be given in return. Failure to return the favor means that the relationship is disrupted. On a colony, sharing is normative and to be expected. But there are additional forms of informal sharing not required by the formal patterns. These include informal friendship pacts, agreements, and reciprocal exchanges between siblings and relatives within the colony and in other colonies. Equality within the peer group is the norm, so when a whole roast duck is served on Sunday noon, the duck must be shared at the table in an equitable manner. One duck is for four persons—always the same four, since persons are always seated in the same position. Informal courtesy requires that two persons eat the breast and better pieces one Sunday, giving the other two the preferred portions the following Sunday. Courtesy also demands that the oldest person begins eating first.

Families as well as individuals may exchange goods and favors for one another. One family may exchange some of its feather allotment for a particular pattern of cloth from another family. Gift giving among friends and relatives takes many forms and is made possible by the small monthly allowances. Gifts are given to a newborn baby. Candy is exchanged on many holidays. Gifts of food are prepared very quickly by a family to be given to relatives in another colony once it is learned that the colony truck or a visitor will be traveling to another colony. Greeting cards at Christmas, Valentine's Day, and Easter are exchanged by young people. Unmarried couples exchange gifts about five times each year on major holidays. Since boys have more opportunity to obtain pocket money than girls, they often give their girlfriends money with which to buy gifts.

Kinship is especially relevant to modes of exchange. Close kin tend to share voluntarily, and it follows that non-kin are excluded from the close circle and are regarded more as strangers. When there is a question of borrowing, brothers living together are on much closer terms than with non-relatives. When several brothers marry into one family, there is an even greater degree of exchange. Painting an apartment is usually done in groups by the unmarried girls who are relatives, and often includes those from another colony. Substitutions for the formal work pattern are usually arranged with close relatives. Persons may obtain a substitute for, but not be excused from, their regular work schedule if they go to town, attend a funeral, or suffer a minor illness. Substituting jobs among the women in *Lehrerhof* is arranged in advance and must be repaid in kind. A specific job cannot be paid back with another job. For childbirth, certain serious illnesses, or an operation, a woman is exempt from having to make up work lost. Whether help is returned depends on the closeness of kin and the amount of work performed.

Negative reciprocity, the most impersonal sort of exchange, is the attempt to get something for nothing, often with pressure or guile, and is directed toward net utilitarian advantage. Among peasant societies it is often the normal thing to use strange means of seizure, including theft, haggling, and witchcraft when trading with foreign peoples. Among Navaho people, for example, Kluckhohn (1949) reports that morality is contextual rather than absolute, so that lying is not always and everywhere wrong. The rules vary with the circumstances. Among Hutterites, any tendency toward negative reciprocity is tempered by their Christian beliefs. Yet, Hutterites have been resented by shopkeepers and merchants for their sharp bargaining and parsimonious attitude. Here again, colonies vary a great deal in their practices but a few illustrations will demonstrate the pattern.

In their world view and in their history the Hutterites have held a negative attitude toward merchandising and trading. Trading is specifically forbidden: "We allow none of our members to do the work of a trader or merchant, since this is a sinful business . . . (Rideman 1950:126). Goods may be improved through human labor, as had been done in a variety of crafts by the colonists in Moravia, but "to buy and sell again, as merchants and traders do, is sin." It is wrong in the Hutterite view because it creates profit by the factor of scarcity and defrauds those in need. The product is made more expensive and "the poor man is made a bondman of the rich." The inability of the Hutterites to appreciate the role of the merchant and the services of the middleman, reminiscent of the peasant classes in the sixteenth century, is reflected in their bargaining relationships. This is not applied equally to all outsiders, but primarily to impersonal, rather than personal, relationships. To buy from wholesalers is therefore not only more reasonable in price but also more consistent with the beliefs. The householder is under strict orders to buy at the most reasonable prices, and not to squander the funds of the church. As a good steward of the colony he must be frugal, but his attitudes may also reflect a certain suspicion of the sinfulness of merchandising. Some of the more discerning merchants have taken the pains to observe differences between colonies in their buying practices instead of criticizing them indiscriminately. Some colonies have responded to the sensitive attitudes of outsiders and do make it a policy to buy from local merchants who can assure them quantities at fair prices. Gift giving serves as a form of compensation for minor deprivations, such as children or a young person pilfering from a neighbor. Outsiders who are friends of the colony, or persons in a position to influence the welfare of the colony, frequently receive gifts of produce. Extortion by outsiders also occurs, and some colonies have suffered financial loss through unfair dealings. Several colonies have lost millions of dollars through unsound ventures in oil and mining stocks.

SUMMARY

Although social patterns are believed to be divinely prescribed and must remain stable, economic and technological practices vary greatly in time and from colony to colony. The production patterns consist of rational and modern methods. Typically large scale agriculture incorporating a diversity of small grains, cattle, dairy, swine, poultry, provides cash income and insures meat and produce for consumption. There is minimal conflict between the religious ideology and the dynamics required for collective utilization of agricultural resources. However, many colonies are becoming more specialized in their agricultural production and some are supplementing agriculture with manufacturing in their own small factories. The high rate of natural increase of the population intensifies the constant need for capital.

Every person capable of working is expected to perform assigned work. Work patterns are clearly specified within age and sex groupings and by formal authority patterns that are firmly supported by informal associations in small groups. Men are more directly engaged in the income-producing phases of colony operations, while women are assigned to family, domestic, and food preparation tasks. There is overall efficient use of labor groups in spite of certain efficiencies resulting from strong authority patterns. Work is considered important, not in terms of individualistic conceptions of time, money, or man hours, but as a means of communal living.

Branching (forming new colonies) is the institutionalized response to biological growth, and the need of the communal system to maintain a small, manageable, face-to-face domestic group. The new colony is usually formed from a single overpopulated "mother" colony. Branching achieves a redistribution of authority, leadership roles, work patterns, economic resources, and balancing of kinship and family influences. Branching enables all Hutterites to experience during their lifetime the recreation of their own society. Every colony requires dynamic adjustments to the changing needs from its beginning until it forms a new colony and as it adjusts to the reduction in the work force caused by the branching process.

The consumption patterns of the society are predetermined by the world view forbidding private ownership of property, rejecting personal pleasure as an end, and an attitude of frugality rather than spending. The conceptions of "need" and "equality" are culturally defined and socially sanctioned by both informal and formal consensus on an intercolony basis. Austerity and simplicity are consciously accepted by the individual as a necessary way of life, in which the carnal desire must be subjugated to the spiritual nature. Although personal and family needs contrast sharply with the North American farm family in clothing, house furnishings, and appliances, the colony as a whole manifests the characteristics of modern, large-scale, capital-oriented agriculture.

The distribution patterns reflect colony conceptions of impartiality and equality in sharing. The amount and kind of goods, determined by the rules of the intercolony association, are distributed according to the age and sex of the individual and according to family size. Although the society is communal and modern in its technology and productive features, its adherence to religious authority prevents a distributive economy based on the maximization of individual wants. Hutterite society is not only communal in production, but also in its consumption and distribution phases. Food is consumed in a communal setting. Clothing and most needs of the individual are distributed through resident household units. Profits realized from the marketplace are held by the corporation for the welfare of the whole colony.

Conceptions of property are clearly shaped by communitarian values, and by the view that material things are unimportant in comparison to spiritual things. To the individual, property means the right to use but not to possess. The formal adult relation to property is one of stewardship but, on the informal level, tools and machines are frequently neglected. Children are not trusted with valued property, and the young adult must learn the appropriate restraints on property use not expected of him as a child. Patterns of reciprocity between individuals and families are made possible through small monthly allowances to individuals from the colony. Kinship is especially relevant in the exchange of gifts, favors, and work substitutions. The Hutterite view of property forbids merchandising or profiteering from mere exchange of goods. Gift giving to outsiders in exchange for colony favors, for minor deprivations, and as a means of expressing appreciation is normative.

4 / Socialization and Family Patterns

Hutterite socialization is a consistent, continuous process building up to two peaks in the life of the individual. Childhood is a preparation for initiation (baptism) into adult life, a period to train the child to identify with the society. Socialization during adulthood reinforces this identification and prepares the individual for death. The pattern of socialization is remarkably consistent from one colony to another, from one family to another, and from one individual to another. The system is sufficiently flexible and rewarding that an unusually high rate of success is observed. Extreme deviancy is rare.

The Hutterites regard themselves as Christian believers maintaining the proper social order and not as a rationalized experiment in communal living. The continued existence of their society is secondary to obedience to God. They are, therefore, willing to become extinct as a society rather than compromise or lose the communal pattern of living, which is equated with the proper worship of God. The child is raised and the adult lives by a social pattern believed to be divinely ordained, apart from any cause and effect relationship that might be evident to an anthropologist or a worldly observer.

The function of the nuclear family is to produce new souls and to care for them until the colony takes over the greater responsibility. At all points in the socialization activity, the family supports the colony. Until the mid-1960's there seemed to be virtually no limits to the number of children a couple might have except those set by nature. Having children is supported by their world view. The prohibition of sex relations before marriage is firmly adhered to—a practice not inconsistent in a society that lives by absolutes in many aspects of life. The demographic study of Eaton and Mayer (1954), covering the period 1874–1950, shows the median age at marriage in 1950 for women to be 22.0 and for men 23.5. Few persons remain unmarried; only 1.9 percent of the men and 5.4 percent of the women over age 30 had never married. Only one divorce and four desertions were reported between 1874 and 1950. The median family size of the completed family was 8.97. Recent trends in family size show a slowing of the growth rate. (Bolt and Roberts 1980) By 1980 the average age of marriage had risen to 24.9 for women and 26.0 for men. In 1971 fifteen percent of the women over 30 were still single and fertility rates among Hutterite women had declined with the drop in crude birth rates mirroring the drop observed for all Canadians. (Laing 1980, Ingoldsby and Stanton 1988.) Hutterite family size is variously estimated at five to just under seven.

Intrafamily relationships are very important to the individual, for these relationships are the first ones learned by the child and will remain the primary ones throughout life. Hutterites say, *Blut ist kein Wasser* (Blood is not water), meaning that blood ties are of utmost importance and not to be taken lightly. Ego feels closer to some relatives than to others due to a variety of factors: similar age and interests, frequency of contact, and marriage ties. Ego's main relationships are with parents, siblings, grandparents, uncles, aunts, and cousins. In line with the earlier discussion of male and female subcultures, women feel closer to the relatives of their mother, especially the mother's sisters, than to the relatives of their father. Men identify more closely with the relatives of their father than with those of their mother. Boys are named after their fathers and uncles, while girls are usually named after their mothers and their aunts.

Throughout the life of the individual it is the responsibility of the whole society, not just the family, the school, the employers, or chance acquaintances to help socialize all the members. "We observe and watch over one another . . . telling each his faults, warning, and rebuking with all diligence" (Rideman 1950: 131–132). Or as one preacher explained, "It is good to live in community, for here there are always one hundred eyes watching you." The group has developed a highly institutionalized and effective system of formal education. The major levels of formal education are kindergarten *(Klein-Schul),* German school *(Gross-Schul),* Sunday school *(Suntag-Schul* or

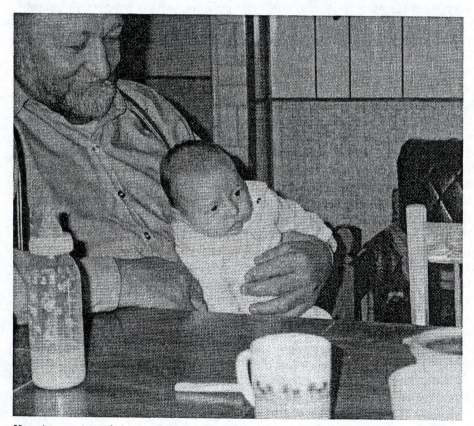

Hutterite parenting includes not only both parents but also grandparents.

Kinder-Schul), baptismal instruction, and the daily evening sermons *(Gebet).* These levels of education correspond to the age sets (described in Chapter 2).

HOUSE CHILDREN: BIRTH TO TWO YEARS

The Hutterites are opposed to any means of birth control. However, family size is declining and they will follow the advice of physicians and permit some family limitation for reasons of health. Hutterites teach that as Christians they are not to interfere with the giving of life nor the taking of life—that is God's prerogative. Within marriage children are gifts from God. There is no institutional recognition of pregnancy; no special costume is worn by the pregnant woman, nor is there any modification in her work program. Informally the women help one another if one of them does not feel well, and some husbands give their wives some extra assistance when they are pregnant. The women say that the harder you work during pregnancy, the healthier your baby will be. Generally, pregnancy is ignored by everyone.

In the United States where hospital costs are high, most Hutterite babies are born in the parents' apartment. The mother is assisted by a female relative and the midwife. In Canadian provinces where the Hutterites are covered by a hospitalization plan, childbirth usually takes place in a hospital. Barring actual illness or obvious complications, the mothers have little or no prenatal medical care. In contrast with the lack of emphasis on pregnancy and on the actual birth, much emphasis is placed on the postpartum woman. The relief from colony responsibilities and the full-time help of a mature woman are given to the mother, not to the baby. Ideally, the woman's own mother comes from her home colony to care for her daughter. If her mother is dead or too old, an older sister is the second choice and any married sister is a third; beyond that the female relative to whom the new mother feels closest is called for assistance. During the postpartum period, the mother is cared for and mothered at the same time that she cares for and mothers her baby. The new mother does not leave her apartment. Her nurse feeds and cares for her and her house children, does all her family work and even sleeps with her at night, helping her twenty-four hours a day. During this period, the colony members and relatives from neighboring colonies come to visit the mother and to see the new baby. The visitors are given a delicious zwieback that is baked for the new mother. For the first five weeks, in addition to the zwieback and the regular colony meals, the new mother is served omelets, rich chicken soups, milk puddings, and chicken roasted in butter, which are prepared especially for her by the diet cook. The length of this period of complete care and dependency varies. Most mothers are anxious to return to colony participation, and as soon as their caretaker leaves they begin to eat "with the people." The integration back into the work pattern is institutionalized. Among the *Darius-Leut,* on the first Monday after the baby is six weeks old, the mother starts to help wash the dishes in the kitchen; on the Monday after the baby is eight weeks old, she does the milking, and if her team makes noodles she helps; when the baby is ten weeks old, she bakes for the colony and hoes in the garden if it is that season of the year. When the baby is thirteen weeks old, she cooks for the colony and is now "back in orbit" as one woman expressed it.

The care given the new mother is not only part of her continuing socialization but also affects the early socialization of the baby. During the first four weeks of life, his mother is able to devote herself exclusively to the infant's care. The Hutterites consider the neonatal child to be demanding and vulnerable, but at the same time a great joy and a pleasure to care for. The mother, who is used to being away from her children for several hours each day, finds the baby, which has in no way adjusted to the dictates of society, quite demanding. But she is confident of her ability to supply his needs and enjoys nurturing the completely dependent baby. The baby wears a cap on his head, is swaddled with a blanket wrapped over his clothes, and is tied into a firm, straight bundle with a narrow cord woven just for this purpose. Swaddling is said to make the baby easier to handle and play with (that is, less easily injured). A red ribbon may be tied onto the baby. Some say that this protects the baby from the evil eye; others, that it keeps the baby from being fussy, from having colic, or that it just gives general protection. Even though the efficacy of the red cord is not believed by all, its use indicates the vulnerability attributed to small babies. Both swaddling and the red ribbon are given up by the time the mother returns to full colony participation. Today these practices are falling into disuse. When the child is four weeks old, the mother's caretaker leaves, and for two more weeks the mother is relieved of colony work. Although she usually eats in the colony dining room and manages her other family responsibilities, she still has extra time to devote to the baby. The baby's schedule becomes adjusted to that of the colony, the mother leaves the child during church service and during the adult meals. As she participates more fully in the colony work program, the pattern of the child's life meshes more closely with that of the colony. The temporal pattern of colony life determines the time of feeding, playing, sleeping, and being left alone.

Nursing is accepted as a matter of fact by Hutterite mothers. No special help or modification in colony schedule is given the nursing mother other than the reduced workload for the first three months. Nursing periods are short, rarely longer than ten minutes, and pacifiers are widely used. Most babies are nursed for about a year or until the mother becomes pregnant again. Occasionally, babies are not weaned until they enter kindergarten. A few mothers only give their babies formula. Religious training begins with the introduction of solid food into the baby's diet (sometime between three weeks and three months). The mother folds the baby's hand in hers and prays with the infant before and after feeding. Religion is already a ritual, a formal activity and a social activity. It is intimately associated with food. Babies under a year will clasp their hands in the prayer position when hungry and food is being carried in. At night, when the baby is put into the crib, the parent says the first children's prayer aloud to her as she is laid down.

Ich bin klein,	I am a little child
Mein Herz ist rein	My heart is pure
In Jesu Namen	In Jesus' name
Schlaf ich ein.	I go to sleep.
Die lieben Engelein,	The beloved Angels
Werden meine Wächter sein.	Will watch over me.
Amen.	Amen.

The prayer is invariably recited whether the baby is still awake or already asleep. Toilet training begins early, often by three months, always by the time the child can sit alone. Many children do not wear diapers after they are six months old, even though they often are not fully trained until they are in kindergarten. Prekindergarten children who are able may attend to their toilet needs outside if they show a little discretion in choosing a spot and do not soil or shed their clothes. When the children start kindergarten they begin going to the toilet without help.

Everyone in a Hutterite colony loves a baby. Children of both sexes will crowd around a baby to play with her and gently vie for the privilege of holding or caring for a tiny baby. A child as young as two will be rewarded by being allowed to hold a baby. When the adults are not working, the babies are always held. After supper, in a group of men sitting around informally discussing colony affairs, one or two will be seen holding babies on their laps; a grandfather may hold two or three children on his. Adult Hutterites, colony members, visitors, and everyone who passes a very young child gives him cheerful attention. The baby is spoken to, picked up, tickled, played with. However, when it is time for church or for the adult meal, the baby is unceremoniously placed in her crib and the parents walk out. Thus, from the time the infant is seven weeks old, he or she alternates between being in a socially stimulating environment and being completely alone in the crib. By the time a child is old enough to climb out of the crib or does not generally sleep during the time the mother is away, the toddler is either watched by a babysitter or taken to an apartment where an adult is at home. This may be a grandmother, or a crippled aunt; in some colonies the toddlers may be left with the head preacher, for he eats his meals in his apartment and therefore can keep an eye on the children while the parents have their breakfast.

A "good" baby has two major attributes. The baby sleeps a lot, at least during colony work periods, and will go to anyone. In other words, the baby does not disrupt the colony time schedule and accepts all colony members. A child is believed to be completely innocent until she is observed to hit back or to pick up a comb and try to comb her hair. When a child hits back, or knows what a comb is for, their level of comprehension is believed to be sufficiently high that they can be disciplined. Such a child shows both self-will and understanding. When little children quarrel over an object, the object is usually removed. If they are quarreling for another reason, they are often told to kiss one another. Some very young children will hit each other and then immediately hug and kiss one another, thus avoiding adult displeasure by quickly making up. An older house child may be strapped for refusing to go to someone other than her parents, for refusing to share food, or for being noisy and disturbing adults. He may be slapped for putting garbage in the wrong receptacle, flicked on the head or pinched for getting in the way of someone older than he, either a child or an adult. Sometimes there is an attempt, usually unsuccessful, to frighten her into good behavior. If she is teasing the geese, someone will pick up a hissing, snapping goose and chase the child with it in an effort to frighten her away. Although the house child is disciplined quickly and frequently, he is considered entertaining and is petted, played with, and desired.

Hutterite mothers almost never take their house children with them when they are doing colony work. "We say that the air in the kitchen is bad for babies." Older children in the kitchen get in the women's way. During the winter the younger house children are left alone in the apartment. If there is pressing colony work at a time when the house children are not napping, the older ones may visit kindergarten or perhaps be looked after by a child who has finished kindergarten but has not yet started English school; or the father will care for the child if his colony work permits. During the summer the older toddlers, especially the boys, accompany their fathers and play near the place where the men are working, usually in the company of the youngest school boys, who watch out for them and take them back to their apartments when the house children's meal bell rings. There is a united effort on the part of the colony, in which the parents actively cooperate, to wean the house child away from his parents and into the group. Most of the activities that are considered especially pleasurable, such as riding in a wagon or on the back of a truck can be enjoyed only if the toddler will leave her parents to join the fun. However, when the little ones are in a group of children, they are often the butt of much teasing.

During these first three years of life the child has passed from complete dependency on his family to a moderate degree of independence. In the summer she wanders quite freely among the longhouses, around the kitchen, and visits the kindergarten. By the time the child is ready to enter kindergarten he has learned, *first,* that the colony takes precedence over the individual. When the bell rings, his mother leaves. *Second,* she has learned that the individual has little control over her environment. Punishment is usually physical, arbitrary, and inconsistent, and, from the child's point of view, often unpredictable. *Third,* although physical insults are unpredictable, the pattern of living is unchanging. Always the same thing is done in the same way at the same time. *Fourth,* the young child has learned to respond positively to every person (Hutterite) who comes within sight or earshot. The child does not complain when handed from one caretaker to another. The child is happy to be with people.

KINDERGARTEN: THREE TO FIVE YEARS

The primary functions of the kindergarten are: (1) To help wean the child from the nuclear family, and to some extent, wean the family from the youngster. (2) To introduce the child to the peer group, and to teach the child how to function in this group. This is of great importance, for the boys will remain in this group throughout their lives, and the girls will grow up in this same peer group. At the age when children in North American society are exerting their growing individuality and developing a concept of self, the Hutterite child is placed in a setting that minimizes treatment as an individual and maximizes identity as a member of a group. (3) The kindergarten teaches the child to respect the authority of the colony in addition to that of parents and babysitters. (4) In the kindergarten the child learns to tolerate a limited, restricted environment. (5) The child is rewarded for a cooperative, docile, passive response to correction and frustration.

The first sharp change of status in the child's life takes place when he or she reaches kindergarten age (two-and-a-half or three, depending on the tradition of the colony). No longer are the children allowed to scream noisily when they are displeased, unhappy, or hurt. They must be quiet around adults, and even cry quietly. The kindergarten child is expected to be more obedient than a house child. A house child will sometimes get out of bed repeatedly in the evening if the parents are in the apartment and have not gone to bed themselves; this behavior is not tolerated in a kindergarten child. Visitors from other colonies do not greet kindergarten children or school children, nor do they say good-bye to them. Adults rarely play with kindergarten children. The status of the kindergarten child within the colony is low. The child has plummeted from a relatively desirable position to the very lowest. The low status is reflected by the quality of the food served in the kindergarten, and by the fact that adults and older children never want the young ones to be around. The kindergarten children are usually shooed away from any gathering, partly because they have not yet learned to be sufficiently quiet and still, but also because anyone older may send them away, and there always seems to be someone who exercises this prerogative. The largest number of threats are used on children of this age, for they are old enough to understand them but not yet old enough to know that the threats are empty. Outside of kindergarten the most frequently heard threats fall into two categories: those teaching that exclusion from the group is unpleasant; and those teaching that beyond the boundaries there lurks danger. Thus a child will be told that he or she will be locked in the hole under the houses or given to a non-Hutterite visitor. If the youngster opens a door, the bee in the closet will sting him, the dog in the (off-limits) barn will bite her, or a bear "outside" will eat her up. When it thunders, the children are told that God is telling the children that they must be obedient.

Parents look forward to the day the child begins kindergarten. A child of this age is considered willful and useless, that is, unable to contribute any labor to the colony. "They can't do anything but memorize." The willfulness is somewhat threatening to a rigidly controlled people, and because the uselessness is no longer combined with complete dependency, it cannot be enjoyed by succoring caretakers. In spite of this, there sometimes appears to be an ambivalent attitude about kindergarten on the part of the mother. One kindergarten mother remarked, "We need the kindergarten, it helps the children and their mothers realize that everyone should know his or her place." In other words, it emphasizes the place of the individual within the whole colony in addition to his place in his nuclear family, and it teaches that the colony position takes precedence over the family position, that colony traditions and regulations supercede the individual wishes of family members.

The formal training of Hutterite children before they enter English school is uniquely and completely Hutterite. The Hutterite system was evolved early in their history (during the second quarter of the sixteenth century), and has been maintained almost entirely unaffected by outside influence. In Europe during the eighteenth century, there were day nurseries where the weaned babies were cared for during the day. These children were between the ages of fifteen or eighteen months and two-and-one-half years. At the age of two-and-one-half the child entered the little school (*Klein-Schul*), which at that time was a boarding school. Since their immigration to North America, the Hutterites have not maintained boarding schools; all children sleep in the apartment of their parents, and the day nursery for the toddlers has been discontinued. *Klein-Schul* is translated here as kindergarten, which is the term the Hutterites use for it when they are speaking in English. However, it should be remembered that the term as used here is not synonymous with the word "kindergarten" as used in the American educational system; it is closer to the concept of "preschool" which is used to refer to the nursery school and the kindergarten.

The kindergarten building is always an integral part of the colony. Ideally, it is near the kitchen and architecturally harmonious with it and the longhouses. The small kindergarten house consists of two or three rooms surrounded by a fenced-in play yard. The house has one room that can be darkened, in which the children take their naps. They rest in assigned places, each child on his own pillow, four to a double bed or arranged along an elevated wooden platform that is built around three walls of the room. There is always a second room that functions as a dining room and, to a limited extent, as a playroom. During the summer the children may be fed in a shed which adjoins the kindergarten house. Each day the kindergarten is supervised by one of two or sometimes three older women. Who shall be chosen as kindergarten mothers is generally not difficult, for traditionally they are the oldest women in the colony still able to work. Occasionally, a younger woman may be assigned, but young women usually have too many house children to be able to stay away from their apartments for so many hours. The kindergarten mothers alternate, each woman taking responsibility for one full day. If one is ill, she generally obtains a substitute from among her relatives. During Sunday church services, a school-age child will supervise the group in order that the adult may attend the service. The kindergarten children arrive before breakfast. They recite their morning prayer, have breakfast, recite another prayer, and sing a hymn. The children recite in unison with their hands folded, either sitting on the bench or kneeling by the bench, rocking rhythmically as they recite. The teacher says the first line, and the children recite it after her. When a whole verse has been memorized, the children and the teacher say it in unison. The children recite very rapidly and the older ones quite loudly. (This is the only occasion on which kindergarten children may raise their voices.) During

The kindergarten is "a time to teach unselfishness."

their years in kindergarten the children learn from ten to twenty-one prayers, depending on the colony, and from twelve to twenty-six hymns. Little if any effort is made to explain the meaning of what is being memorized.

The children eat their dinner, the main meal of the day, at about 10:30 A.M.; then they take a long nap that enables the kindergarten mother to join the adults in the dining room for her dinner. When they awaken from their nap, they are fed a snack. In most colonies they return home about midafternoon, but in some colonies they remain in kindergarten until after their supper at 5:30 or 6:00. The length of the school year varies among the colonies. In spite of the variation in schedule among the three *Leut*, it is obvious that one of the functions of the kindergarten is to free the mothers to do colony work.

Equipment used in the kindergartens in *Lehrerhof* and *Dariushof* is minimal, while the *Schmiedehof* kindergarten is almost as well-equipped as some small community nursery schools. At *Schmiedehof* children are not allowed to bring toys from home, for one of the purposes of kindergarten is to teach the children to play together, to share, and not to have personal property. "This is a time to plant unselfishness and teach the little ones to put self aside." There are no toys in either *Dariushof* or *Lehrerhof* kindergartens because "toys make children fight." However, children may bring a pocket toy from home. The kindergarten mother may occasionally bring a magazine or a catalog for the children. Of all the aspects of the kindergarten education, the indoor play shows the greatest variation among colonies. In *Schmiedehof* the children have an equipped playroom and, although their play is directed and somewhat restricted to the acceptable part of the room, there is considerable freedom of movement and variety of activity. There appears to be an unconscious effort on the part of the teachers to separate the sexes and encourage the acting out of future sex-determined roles. The boys tend to play at one end of the room with the blocks and tractors, the girls at the other with the dishes, table, and dolls. Little girls will play "head cook" and "mother"; the boys play "tractor," "working with animals," and "father." The teacher says there is not much trouble with the little ones fighting because she keeps them busy.

The outdoor play is vigorous, with a great deal of running, jumping, and, when possible, climbing. This play is barely supervised; the kindergarten mother is usually inside cleaning the schoolhouse or sewing and knitting. Most of the play involves gross muscle activity. The children play horse and tractor and chase one another. Occasionally, they will play child and adult and take turns pretending to strap each other. They also fight, but as long as the fighting is quiet, it goes unnoticed by the kindergarten mother. The children may be taken on walks by the kindergarten mother to visit different parts of the colony. They may be taken to see the baby pigs or to look at the new combine, or to the garden where they are allowed to pick and eat any of the vegetables or fruit. Little effort is made to explain to the children what they see or to relate one thing to another. These walks are not thought of as educational experiences but as something pleasant or as a convenience for the kindergarten mother.

Asocial behavior is quickly punished; the children are not allowed to fight, quarrel, or hit; they are not to call one another names or to use "bad words." They may not disobey the person in charge. They may not leave the kindergarten yard. If the children will not share, they are punished. The kindergarten mothers do not take the children's misbehavior personally and it does not make them tense; they assume that children so young have not yet learned how to act and they need punishment to help them learn to avoid misbehavior.

The kindergarten mothers use encouragement, praise, and rewards with the children. The little boys are told to "Eat up! eat up! so you can drive a Massey (tractor)." An older child who has been helpful may be allowed to go with the kindergarten mother to bring the food over from the kitchen. A child who has behaved very well may be the first to be dismissed in the afternoon. The group may be promised a walk if they are good, or a small child may be comforted with a little candy from the kindergarten mother's pocket. Punishment includes scolding, switching, and the use of threats. The kindergarten mothers quite often yell at the children and threaten them with the use of the willow or strap. Some kindergarten mothers feel that a leather strap is too cruel for children and makes them tough without correcting them, and that a willow switch is better. The children are given only one or two switches and those older than four rarely cry. When a three-year-old was crying after being punished, one of the five-year-olds remarked, "We're already tough, we don't cry anymore, only Michael does." (Michael had just begun kindergarten.) The children are never punished vindictively or in anger. Their kindergarten mother who, as the name implies, regards them almost as her own children, is confident that she is helping the children grow into civilized Christians.

The children's adjustment to kindergarten is eased by the fact that they have visited the kindergarten with increasing frequency since they were toddlers, that they know all the other children intimately, and that they have known the kindergarten mothers all their lives. In spite of this, kindergarten requires a real adjustment. The children must go to the kindergarten and stay there for the full day under the supervision of one adult who is not a parent. Children's initial dislike of kindergarten is considered natural and is hardly noticed. To the Hutterites it is obvious that children of this age have stubborn wills that need to be broken; and kindergarten will help teach the children not to be stubborn and willful. As one kindergarten mother explained when she swatted a boy who was licking his boots, "He's only three years old and still very young. He'll need many *Britschen* before his will is broken." Sometimes a child will sit on the kindergarten bench, rocking rhythmically and repeating in a barely audible whisper, "I want my mother, I want my mother, I want my mother." The colony system is consistent, and in a well-managed colony is supported by all the individuals; there is no recourse for the three-year-old but to submit. The child may be frustrated for a while but finally learns that obedience and acceptance are the best policy. The child plays vigorously and with gusto, especially when in the company of other kindergartners removed from the close supervision of any adult or school child.

The impact of the colony on the individual is greatest during the kindergarten years, for of all age groups those in the kindergarten are the most restricted, most regimented, and have the least variation in the program. Physically, the children spend virtually the whole day in one little building and small enclosed yard; they are cared for throughout the day by only one adult. There are no vacations during the school year, except for half-day sessions on weekends and church holidays. This intensive socialization takes place at a psychologically important point in the child's development. Simultaneously, parents and the adult colony members no longer tolerate the range of behavior accorded a baby. The kindergartner can easily interpret these changes as rejection. The kindergartner has fallen to the lowest status group within the colony but has also started the steady, rewarding climb up the steps that lead to full, responsible membership in the colony.

SCHOOL CHILDREN: SIX TO FOURTEEN YEARS

Significant aspects of the socialization of school-age children include the following:

1. Most of the children's day is spent under close supervision by someone in a position of authority—the German teacher, a parent, or a work supervisor. During each day, however, there are periods when the children are working with their brothers or sisters and when the children are unsupervised in their peer group.
2. The groups of brothers and sisters working together within the nuclear family develop patterns of interaction that will continue into adulthood when groups of brothers will be in leadership positions in the colony and when, it is to be hoped, sisters will marry into the same colony, where they can help one another.
3. Every day there are brief periods when the school children are completely free from authoritarian direction and can function as a self-contained peer group, working out relationships that will last into adulthood. During the school years the children learn to function both within the sibling group and within the peer group. They learn how to adjust their dual membership as the two groups overlap, interact, and supplement one another. The two configurations persist, with traditional modification, until the peer-group embraces the whole colony.
4. The school-age children are taught unquestioning obedience to Hutterite authority—their parents, teacher, the colony, to any Hutterite older than they, and to Hutterite traditions and teachings. If in the weakness of childhood they do not obey, they are taught to accept their punishment meekly.
5. They are not taught to discipline themselves, deciding what is right and following their own concept of truth; rather, they are taught to do what they are told and that those in authority will watch over them, punish, and protect them.
6. The children do not develop a strong sense of guilt. Because it is natural for children to sin, and because children are not responsible for their sin, it is not "their fault" that they misbehave. Children's actions need to be directed through praise and punishment by those over them.
7. The school children master the basic ritual of Hutterite life. They abide by the rules because they are told to and they must be obedient. The children learn the verbal expression of the belief system. They must memorize the material, but it is not yet expected that they will really internalize the more difficult aspects of the beliefs.
8. The children learn to accept their proper position in the society. One German teacher begins each day's lesson with, "Dear children, content yourself gladly with a lowly place. . . . Do not interfere in things that are not your concern." The children learn to accept many frustrations passively. They learn to interpret teasing as attention, to enjoy hard physical labor, to begin to appreciate life uncluttered by material objects, and to accept the cleansing process of pain and punishment with a kind of pleasure.

During the height of the Hutterite development in Europe, the *Gross-Schul* was a boarding school and was responsible for the children twenty-four hours a day. Today, all children sleep in their parents' apartments at night and a large part of the time that

The German school, teacher and pupils.

formerly was spent in German school is now spent attending English school. However, the children start German school before starting English school. Among the *Schmied-Leut* the children enter German school at five, so they have at least one year in the German school before entering the English school. Among the *Lehrer-Leut* there is a subdivision of the German school called *Schulela*, which the children attend from their sixth birthday until they enter English school at about seven. There are regular class hours for the *Schulela* students that meet during English school sessions. All children are taught their German letters and read German before learning English. During the period that the children attend only German school, they eat in the children's dining room under the supervision of the German teacher, attend German school when it is in session, go to Sunday school, church, and the evening service. While the children are in English school, the few younger ones help with the prekindergarten babies, or accompany their fathers around the colony. They may not go with their mothers when the women are doing colony work.

The school child can contribute some labor to the smooth functioning of the colony and can help within the nuclear family. They work as baby sitters for the house children and kindergartners, ordering their young charges around and punishing disobedience. School children are not greeted formally by Hutterite visitors, nor are they introduced to adults. There are slight changes in dress when the child enters German school.

German school is taught by a married man who has been selected for his job by the *Gemein*. The position is equal in importance to any other department leadership position. Often the German teacher is on the colony council, although not invariably.

It is considered an advantage for him to be on the front bench because then he can easily watch the children and note any misbehavior. The school children must sit very still and be absolutely quiet during church. If a child should fall asleep, he is not scolded, for he is still observing the ritual by being in church and being quiet. The German school mother is frequently the wife of the German school teacher (especially among the *Darius-Leut*), or she may be an older woman who is appointed to the position by the council. She helps to supervise the children's meals, serves them, and teachers manners. She also teaches the girls how to clean the dining room, set the tables, wash, dry, and put away their dishes. She has no responsibility to teach any of the religious material nor does she give permission, assign jobs, and punish. She assists the German teacher and instructs the school girls in their female work roles, teaching them the pattern of work rotation that will organize their colony work for the remainder of their lives.

German school is usually taught in the English schoolhouse. Every day the children assemble in the dining room for morning prayers and breakfast. From the moment they assemble until after supper in the evening, the children are either under the direction of the German teacher or are technically released by him to do specific work such as baby-sitting, helping with chores, or attending English school. During the English school year the children meet before and after English school from an hour to an hour-and-a-half. They meet a half-day on Saturday and all day during vacations or when the English teacher is sick. During this time they practice writing German script, read German, recite their memory verses from Hutterite hymns, the Book of Psalms, the New Testament, or a biblical history book. The German teacher admonishes them about their beliefs and even more about their behavior. Here, rules are announced to the children, and those who have broken the rules are punished. For example, the teacher may announce that the children are not to touch the car of any English person who comes to the colony. If at a later time any child is seen climbing

The English school, teacher and pupils.

on the car or playing inside it, he or she is reported to the German teacher who gives the offender the standard number of straps. This is usually three on the palm of the hand for the first offense or for a minor infringement. If a child lies about what he did, he gets two more. If the offense merits greater punishment, he is turned over to the bench. During the long, cold winters the children wear so many layers of thick cotton flannel that when a switch is used it is more the disgrace than the physical discomfort that causes the pain.

In addition to teaching the school children to pray together, the German school teaches them to work together. Often the German teacher is the gardener or the husband of the gardener. This is a convenient arrangement, for the school children regularly help in the garden during the summer when they have no English school. The potatoes are often dug by the school children, and cucumbers and other vegetables are sorted for sale. When the children have worked especially hard or especially well, the whole group is rewarded. After they have spent the morning gathering potatoes, each child may be given a chocolate bar at dinner.

Except when they are baby-sitting, all the children's work is closely supervised, for children are not expected to be able to work on their own. Each girl has an assigned task in the dining room clean-up routine for one week at a time, but some jobs are more popular than others, and the children race to get these. If the girl to whom the job has been assigned does not stand up for her right or enlist the help of the German school mother to defend her place, she will have to perform one of the less popular tasks. This rushing to grab a preferred job functions to hurry the girls from the table to work, for the easiest way to defend one's job is to get there first. Jockeying for a favored position is expected among the school children, but it would be beneath the dignity of anyone old enough to eat in the adult dining room.

When the German school is in formal session the teacher holds a willow switch or a leather strap in his hand throughout most of the period. This functions more as a symbol of authority than as a ready implement for discipline, as a sceptre rather than a whip. When, for example, the preacher took over the German school and called it into session outside of regular school hours, he picked up the willow and sat down at the front of the room. The children went quickly to their assigned places and sat expectantly, waiting to be told what to do. It was not merely the presence of the preacher that elicited this reaction, for he had been in the room for several minutes talking to individual children and watching them play jacks and run around the school room before he decided to take over.

The naturalness of discipline in the German school is illustrated by the following incident. Children are not allowed to speak unnecessarily during meals. (One can realize the need for this rule watching two adults serve and control fifty-six school-age children who must pray, be served, eat, and pray again—all this within fifteen minutes.) During breakfast one day two of the little girls were whispering and giggling. As the German teacher walked past he switched the noisier child with his rod. Her skirt was hanging over the edge of the bench and instead of striking the child, he hit the bench, knocking his switch under the table. The girls quickly picked it up and sat on it, hiding it under their long skirts. For the rest of the meal, the teacher was without his switch. This was considered a humorous incident by the teacher as well as all the children. A single switch or being flicked on the head in the dining room is primarily a means for directing the child's attention to his eating without having to speak to him, rather than a real punishment. The dining room is always to be quiet, except when the children are singing, and even the teacher and the German school mother do very little talking during the meal.

One of the functions of German school is to continue to teach the child to accept punishment without resistance and without anger. The German teacher uses traditional colony methods of punishment. An erring child is spoken to, is made to stand by his desk, must sit on the front bench, may have to kneel, may be sent to stand in the corner, or must come forward and receive three straps on his or her hand. All these punishments function primarily to remove the child from the group and shame him in front of his peers. Other punishment may be given in front of the group or after German school is dismissed, depending on the discretion of the teacher. For repeated offenses a child is first spanked with a switch and, if he persists, with a leather strap. If these methods do not work, the child is placed with the youngest children in the German school until the child is ashamed and claims by proper conduct his age-determined place in the hierarchy. Girls are rarely punished physically after the age of about eleven. Praise is used to encourage all the children, even the slowest.

Children's native abilities are taken into account, and children who are slow learners are given less material to memorize. German school is "ungraded" in the modern sense, with the children progressing at their own speeds. There are no grades or formal levels, rather an accepted sequence of material to be learned. First they earn to recognize their German letters both in Gothic print and Gothic script; they learn to recognize numbers. Then they learn to write the letters and the numbers. Next they are taught to recognize common syllables; these elements they combine together to form words. After several months they are reading and writing the medieval German script. Throughout their school years they practice handwriting, memorize prayers, hymns, Bible stories, the catechism, and episodes of Hutterite history. The children also learn the directions of the compass, measurement equivalents, and how to write to 10,000. The children are taught to work efficiently; they know what to do, how to do it, but they are never given an opportunity to ask if it should be done at all.

Within the system there is no room for doubt. The intellectual content of the German school curriculum is but a small part of the total learning that takes place in the school. The primary function of the German school is to teach the Hutterite children the ritual of life, which applies primarily to two different areas. The first is ritual that insures the smooth social functioning of the group in all the details of everyday interaction. The second class of ritual reduces the fear of death and physical injury. The children in the German school learn primarily the first type of ritual, although the second is not neglected. Psychological studies of Hutterite adolescents show they are not frightened by threats to their bodily integrity, although there are in fact many instances of physical injury. These are not anticipated, nor do they serve as a source of worry.

One of the tasks of the German teacher is to teach his charges table manners. They learn to eat with a knife and fork in addition to a spoon, to serve themselves from the nearest quarter of the serving plate, the oldest taking the first helping. The table rules that the children memorize are very similar in form (rhymed couplets) and content to those widely circulated in Europe during the fifteenth and sixteenth centuries. These rules, dictating how they are to behave at the table, are memorized and recited in unison. (Appendix B)

Within the larger context of ritual the children learn the verbal content of their religion. They will internalize the theological and moral content when they seek baptism. At this stage in development, the child is taught to avoid punishment at the hands of supervising adults. Children memorize the material because they must be obedient; only when they grow older are they expected to understand the concepts they recite. This pattern of learning is consistent with that observed in other cultures having an oral tradition. Wisdom, which is preeminently social rather than technological, is first memorized, then understood.

School children learn a great deal about the authority structure of their society and how to live comfortably within it. They have internalized the Hutterite hierarchy that gives precedence to age, but they have also learned that the authority of each individual is limited. Therefore, the child knows when and whom he must obey and what orders can be safely ignored. If the children are disturbing the young pigs and an adult tells them to stop, they pay little attention other than to stay beyond reach of the reproving adult. If the pig boss tells the children to "get away," they leave.

The German teacher's role is defined by tradition; his work is watched over by the council members and noted by all the members of the church. Concerning his task, one German teacher wrote: "I feel that the greatest challenge in my work is to put a good religious foundation under the children, so that they may become respectable and honorable members of the *Gemein*. I always like to think of them as young tender plants in the Garden of the Lord, where the school teacher's duty is to trim, weed, and water as he finds it necessary. Of course, I realize that neither the plant nor the waterer can achieve anything without the Lord's blessing."

The peer group which functions beyond the supervision of the German teacher and the child's nuclear family, contributes to the socialization of the individual. Every day, while the adults are eating, the children of the colony who are younger than fifteen are left with no adult supervision. During these few minutes the children are virtually free to settle their own disputes and to apply peer group pressure to deviants.

Boys and girls are taught to play differently. When a group of girls played leapfrog, ignoring their long skirts, the preacher picked up a switch and walked toward the scattering group, admonishing them firmly with "girls don't play that way." In some colonies the sisters in each family have an assigned playhouse. This may be an abandoned shed or an attic corner or even an infrequently used room in one of the houses. Here they spend hours playing with each other and with the girls from other families. Usually, each little girl brings a doll out from hiding under her skirt and plays house, happily knowing that she will be undisturbed by the preacher, who would throw the doll in the trash were she to flaunt it. Occasionally, the girls will play that they are "English" women, wearing funny clothes, strutting about, and talking loudly. On the very rare occasions when one of the girl's brothers is allowed into the playhouse, the children may play "doctor," drawing realistic incisions complete with sutures on one another's arms. The oldest sister in each family keeps the key to the playhouse, and children are free to exclude the children with whom they do not wish to play. Boys are customarily excluded; among the girls, the play groups constantly shift and there is almost always at least one girl who temporarily is being locked out of the favored playhouse. Sometimes the girls divide into cliques, each clique using one playhouse. The cliques, so separate in their play, quickly unite to confront the boys or an adult. Most of the girls' play is near the longhouses and the center of the colony. In contrast, the boys range much farther in their play. The boys are more individualistic and often will work or play alone. The girls demand detailed conformity within the clique or the dissenter is excluded. Only by adjusting completely to the group may a girl remain to play.

Much of the children's play is physically vigorous and often rough. They run and chase and climb. They fight hard, quickly and quietly. They vie with one another, showing no physical fear, jumping off high places or pushing one another in front of the tractor. Adults ignore the children's dangerous play; they are busy, and the children are the German teacher's responsibility. If an adult should not like the play, he might yell at the children, who would momentarily scatter. If he were really bothered, he might tell the German teacher who, if in agreement would make the children stop their play. Normally, however, no one notices how the children play if they are quiet. School children play such games as "whistle when it hurts," in other words, games that are exercises in discomfort and endurance. The free play of school children reinforces community values: the children learn to ignore physical discomfort and fear of injury and to minimize the importance of the body; the changing play groups teach the unpleasantness of being excluded.

During the school years the children identify closely with their respective peer groups. When the group works hard or some of the members do especially well, everyone in the group is rewarded. When most of the group misbehaves, everyone is scolded. The child learns not only that the behavior of the group directly affects the rewards and punishment received, but also that peer-group solidarity can protect one from "outsiders" (adults) and from punishment. Transgression can go unnoticed if no one reports it. If no one will tattle on another, often the transgressor is protected. It generally requires too great an effort to punish every child. However, the school children learn that their own peer group can punish even more severely than an adult. The rules of the colony can sometimes be circumvented. Even more often, the rules of the family can be ignored; but the child cannot ignore his own peers.

All assigned baby sitters in the colony are school children between the ages of six and fourteen. Usually, only girls are assigned to a specific family but, if needed, boys may be assigned; however, all boys baby-sit informally within their nuclear families. The primary functions of the baby sitters are to keep their charges quiet and out of the adults' way and to protect them from serious injury. The sitters enjoy being able to boss their charges and to punish them, but they do not like the work involved. The baby sitters are highly responsible in that while they are in charge, they never leave their charges unattended. When there is a conflict, the older child is supported against the younger. During the summer there is some exchange of baby sitters among colonies. Older school girls may be sent to help a sister or an aunt who has married into another colony. These girls help with the young children and with the family work and attend German school. Boys of this age do not perform comparable exchange work: it is not considered right for a young boy to be away from his father or his home colony. For a girl it does not matter, because she will probably leave her home colony when she is married.

A child is never punished by depriving him or her of food. When an English teacher kept a child in school during the dinner period, the German teacher went to the school house and got the child, firmly explaining to the English teacher that children, no matter how they have behaved, need to be fed. Work is never used as a punishment, for there is no colony work that is categorized as unpleasant and everyone must be willing to do any type of work assigned. Privileges are not withheld from a naughty child; if the group goes on an excursion to help butcher sheep or brand cattle, every child can go. If it is his or her turn to visit another colony when the truck is going, the child may go no matter how recently he has misbehaved. When children are observed to be misbehaving, they are ignored or punished immediately; if misbehavior is reported to the German teacher or father, each child is punished at the first opportunity. If a child is strapped by his father, he is comforted by his mother the moment it is over; if his mother is not present, his father may comfort him after strapping him. It is believed that the punishment removed the misbehavior, and the child is fully accepted without having to atone further. When a child is punished in front of school children with no parent present, there is generally no comforting unless it is at the end of the session and the child can return home. Occasionally, if a parent is considered to be too lax with a child, the father may be asked by the colony to punish the child at home, or in the presence of the council. There is a basis for this practice in the biblical story of Eli, recounted in one of the Hutterite sermons on child training. If a father, especially one in a high colony position, feels that his child is not being properly disciplined, he will take over the task. In one colony the English teacher was almost unable to manage one of the larger boys. She did not report this to the German teacher, but the boy's father learned of the problem. The next morning he came into the classroom with the child, sat on one of the church benches during the opening exercises and then asked the teacher, "Has John been misbehaving in school?" The teacher answered, "Yes." The father went to his son's desk, turned him over it, strapped him in front of the children, and then he walked out. Punishment is considered part of the pruning that is needed to shape the individual to fit into colony life.

Children are expected to misbehave when they are unwatched, for that is believed to be their nature. These same children are expected to grow into responsible colony members. Misbehavior during childhood does not endanger the child's future reputation nor foretell an unsuccessful adulthood. Throughout their lives, the expectation is that children will become more responsible, highly socialized persons. School-age children must accept their place in the social structure of the colony, respecting those older than they and caring for those younger. It is not their responsibility to care for themselves, nor to discipline themselves. The same children who are completely responsible in their assigned colony jobs may get into serious mischief during unsupervised play with their peers. Thus, if several children play with fire, accidentally setting the barn aflame, they are punished but not made to feel guilty, for lack of judgment and misbehavior are natural to children. It is not the responsibility of the individual but of the adults and of the system to protect the children from their natural instincts.

To summarize, the Hutterites emphasize nurturant behavior, both within the family and among colonies. Sharing and affection are encouraged. Huntington (1987) reports elsewhere that when two children grab for an object, they are often quickly separated and cuddled by a caretaker rather than being punished. Thus, people are more important than things. Nurturance is never withheld. No one is ever deprived of food, either meals or treats, and there is always someone to comfort the individual after punishment.

Children and adults are taught to nurture each other, to punish one another when deserved, but not to compete. After a child receives several blows of the strap, the child is always cuddled, either by the person giving the punishment or by someone who observed it. This pattern is pervasive. Punishment and love are juxtaposed and mixed. A house child will hit a playmate and then kiss him. Baby sitters will mix cuddling and hurting. Transgression must be punished, but rather than being vindictive, it is "cleansing."

Mature Hutterites are nonaggressive, not self-centered or assertive, and within the colony they are altruistic, nurturant, and responsible. Spiro's (1858) description of Kibbutz-reared children as introverted, hostile, insecure, and having feelings of insecurity does not fit the Hutterites.

YOUNG PEOPLE: AGE FIFTEEN TO BAPTISM

Childhood comes to an end with the fifteenth birthday. The young Hutterite leaves the children's dining room and is said to be *bei die Leut,* with the people. The *Mandle* (boy) has become a *Buah* (young man); the *Dindla* (girl) has become a *Die-en* (young woman).

On the eve of his or her fifteenth birthday the young person goes alone to the German teacher. For weeks the child has been counting the days until his or her birthday with eager anticipation, but the last few days the child frequently becomes apprehensive about the impending change. The older ones may tease the child, saying the German teacher will give him (or her) a whipping. The child does not really believe the teasing, but the change in life patterns is both enticing and frightening. The German teacher exhorts the child to be good, to work hard, to show good manners, and to do quickly and pleasantly everything that an older person asks him or her to do. On leaving the German school, the individual accepts the responsibility for saying his evening and morning prayers without supervision. The young person is given a catechism and several Hutterite books for personal use.

The child takes his or her place in the adult dining hall, for he or she is now "one of the people." The boy sits with the men, occupying the "lowest" position at the table. The girl sits with the women in a similar relationship. She must wait on the men, should they rap for anything during mealtime. The young person does assigned colony work with peers or with adults of the same sex. A fifteen-year-old no longer does the work of children such as baby-sitting, gathering potatoes or cleaning up the colony grounds and no longer attends English school or German school. He or she is greeted with a handshake by visiting Hutterites and is allowed onto the fringes of adult social life.

The young person is in a transitional stage from childhood to adulthood. The colony recognizes both aspects of his personality. Physically, he is considered to be an adult who is capable of hard work and of working with adults. Religiously, he is considered to be a child who must attend Sunday school and must memorize the weekly verses. Emotionally, he or she may vacillate, and this period is sometimes called "the in-between years" or "the foolish years," meaning that the loyalties of the individual have not completely crystallized. Some disregard of colony mores is expected during this period, but moodiness or poor work performance is not tolerated. A good young person is "always obedient and never talks back."

Soon after their fifteenth birthday, but gradually and at the colony's convenience, they are given various gifts that reflect a change of status and are needed in their new role. Both boys and girls are given a locked wooden chest in which to keep their personal belongings. In some colonies a boy may choose a desk instead of a chest; and a girl may choose a dresser. The boy is given cloth for good suits and shirts; the girl receives material for dresses. Boys are given work tools that they are responsible for keeping in good working condition: a spade, a pitchfork, a hammer, a saw, and in some colonies a spoon with the individual's name inscribed on it. The girls receive tools that they will care for and use for colony work: a scrub pail, a paint brush, a hoe, kitchen knives, a broom, knitting needles, and perhaps a rolling pin. If extra labor is required after their own work is completed, girls may assist with boys' work such as haying or driving a tractor.

For two years the young person is in an apprentice position. The young person is not given responsibility for an expensive machine or for work that, if it should go wrong, would cause a great deal of inconvenience or much money lost. A boy is usually assigned the responsibility for a tractor at about the age of seventeen or eighteen. It is his to use for the colony, to care for and keep in good condition. Formerly, boys of this age were given a team of horses to train for field work. At the age of seventeen, girls begin to take their turn baking and cooking for the colony, being responsible for all the food prepared or all the baking done during the week. The boys and girls of the in-between years constitute a mobile labor force that can be used throughout the colony as needed (in jobs suitable to their sex), and they also may be sent to other colonies to help during a time of need or stress. The boys in this group supply most of the hard labor and enjoy the opportunity to demonstrate their strength and stamina.

The young person is subject to the control and influence of the colony, his family, and his peer group. The influences of these three groups are less well-integrated during the years preceding baptism than at any other period. Because the areas of control are more diversified, the young person has slightly more freedom. His work is under the control of the colony, although there may be some tendency to let the son work with the father and the girl work with her mother or with a sister. While working, the boy is under the direction of the departmental director, who may send him off the colony on an errand. His religious development is under the direction of the

German teacher, who is in charge of Sunday school. In areas of moral and social behavior the young person is primarily the responsibility of the German teacher in some colonies, while in other colonies he is the responsibility of the preacher. Depending on the degree of infringement, the transgression may be handled by the German teacher, the preacher, or the council. Permission to leave the colony, other than to do an errand needed for work, is granted by the German teacher among the *Darius-Leut* and the preacher among the *Lehrer-Leut*. It is not granted by the parent. The colony permits dating among the young people, although a specific family may forbid it. If a young person is dating someone of whom the colony disapproves, such as a first cousin or the English school teacher, the German teacher or the preacher speaks to him; if he is dating someone whom his family dislikes, it is a family responsibility and the colony is not involved. Both the colony and the family expect a certain amount of deviant behavior. Much of this takes place within the peer group, who participate together in forbidden activities of singing English songs and playing mouth organs, but the peer group tolerates only certain approved activities. If an individual deviates too radically, he is excluded by his peers.

Within the family, the young person is no longer grouped with the school children. Parents take a greater interest in his or her wants and needs and identify somewhat more closely with the young person. The relationship is still completely hierarchial, but now that the child has become a person and the German teacher is no longer responsible for virtually all the child's waking hours, the parents concern themselves more with their child's free time. "A wise mother has always an odd job for the idle hands of her daughter." Parents have almost complete veto power over the marriage of their children, and they start early to express interest in this aspect of their children's lives. Among the *Darius-Leut,* physical punishment is not used by the colony representative after a child is fifteen (for girls over twelve, it is not used, other than straps on the hand), but it may be used by the parents; however, in practice, this is not necessary. Among the *Lehrer-Leut* a disobedient daughter may be locked out of the apartment and forced to seek lodging with another family for the night. (The parents know that she will not leave the colony and that other families will give her shelter.) Mothers continue to teach their daughters homemaking skills, and girls of this age often take over the family laundry and do much of the sewing.

The young people in the family support one another. The girls may sew for their brothers, making clothes for them that deviate slightly from the accepted pattern. An adult woman would not make a shirt with a forbidden pocket on it, but a young girl will make such a shirt for her brother (or boyfriend) or will add a pocket to a shirt he already owns. A sister will iron her brother's clothes just the way he likes them. Boys have some opportunities to earn extra money that they may lend or give to their sisters or girlfriend. Brothers in one family frequently will date sisters in another family. Brothers support one another, and sisters support one another during the period of dating and after they are married. It is common to find marriages where several brothers are married to women who are sisters. The cooperative patterns learned in the nuclear family influence the pattern of courtship. Colonies that frequently visit back and forth and exchange work and produce and from whom marriage partners are chosen are usually ones that are closely related by family ties.

Although young people have left German school and English school, their education is continuing. The family continues to teach its sons and especially its daughters skills helpful for colony life. In the religious sphere the formal education of the individual continues, for the young people must attend Sunday school on Sunday afternoon. Sunday school functions to reinforce the sermon and to discipline the young people to listen to the sermon. Although all the German-school children also attend and participate in most of the program, the emphasis of the Sunday-school program is directed to the young people who have finished the colony German school but who have not yet been baptized. The colony punishes young people for moral or social transgression by admonishing them or by making the offender stand in Sunday school. If there has been a gross infringement, the offender may have to stand in the back during the evening service, or for a worse offense, he may have to stand in the back during the Sunday service. For a still worse offense, he may have to stand at the front of the church. This is considered too harsh a punishment for a girl to endure. The attitude toward the punishment is revealed by an older Hutterite, who said, with intense emotion, "He needs to stand there like a 'dumb ox' in front of everybody." The implication was that the erring one would really feel how stupid he had been. An offense for which a boy might have to stand in Sunday school would be for having his hair cut too short or attending a movie. A boy might stand in church for sneaking off the colony and being arrested by the local police for drinking with minors. The Sunday-school program reminds young people of their spiritual status as children who must memorize and recite their lessons correctly at the bidding of their teacher. By physically grouping them with the young children and continuing their ritualistic participation with the school children for religious training, those who are not yet baptized are constantly reminded that they are not yet fully adult. Each week, in effect, they are told, "Although you may look like an adult and work like an adult, really, you are still a child." Sunday school is a place where behavior problems that may arise among the young people can be discussed. The push of society is toward adulthood, even while recognizing and tolerating the childish elements that still remain.

During the work day, both the boys and the girls work with and under the direction of older colony members, but they also work in peer groups: all the young men hay together, all the young girls paint together. Work and social life intermingle, for as they work together they talk together, especially when beyond the hearing of adults. It is considered a privilege to go to other colonies to work, because here too the young people work with their peers and establish new friendships. After supper the peer group expands to include both sexes and visitors of the same age group from other colonies. Frequently, there is no one in their home colony whom a young person can date, because all those of similar age are first cousins; or if there are some to whom one is more distantly related, they may be "going with" someone else.

The intermingling of work, visiting, and dating is illustrated in the following account. On Friday afternoon a truck arrived from a colony in a neighboring province. The driver was a young unmarried man who was related to this colony by marriage and was known to be dating one of the girls in the host colony. She did not know in advance that he was coming, nor did he know that he would be chosen to drive the truck until he was told to get ready. With him, riding inside, was an older woman who was the sister of one of the older men in the host colony. The woman had her youngest child with her, a boy of about nine. She had come to visit her brother. Eight girls came along in the back of the truck, because the host colony had a bumper crop of cucumbers.

The truck arrived too late that Friday to do any picking. Saturday morning the girls picked, but Saturday afternoon everyone needed to prepare for Sunday, so no more cucumbers were gathered. Sunday, the young people were neither allowed to pick vegetables nor to travel; they stayed over Sunday. Early Monday morning they picked more cucumbers before the truck left. The visit enabled the girls to work and also to spend the entire weekend visiting. The girls of the host colony were with the visitors constantly, helping them pick, pack, and showing them around. Who was to stay with whom was easily decided, for each girl stayed with her closest relative. Early in the evening all the young people gathered together and sang Western songs, usually ones with a plaintive tune and many verses telling some sad tale of worldly life; an orphan with no one to care for her, a mother whose only child is killed after her husband has deserted her, a dutiful son killed in a war. Later in the evening the young people separated into couples. The boys in the host colony decided who would date whom. The oldest boy has first choice and the others decide in order of age. If a boy has a girlfriend at another colony, he will indicate that he does not want to date. If it is known that one couple is going together, this is, of course, accepted. If a visiting girl does not want to date, or does not want to date a specific person, she says "No." If boys and girls do not know one another, they tend to pair up by age. The younger boys at the host colony will be included in the group of young people but probably will not have a date, for the older boys will have claimed all the visiting girls.

Dating generally begins when the child becomes a young person. Occasionally and surreptitiously, it may begin earlier in colonies where there are children more distantly related than first cousins. Some parents do not allow their daughters to date until they are seventeen or eighteen, or even older. There is a considerable individual variation among the young people; some date whenever and whomever they may, others go only with one person for a long period of time. It is not unusual for courtship to last five or six years. Whether or not a young person is dating, each is included in the mixed peer group activity and remains absolutely loyal to the group.

The peer group is of supreme importance, for within it virtually all the young person's social life takes place, and many of his working hours are spent with his or her same-sex peer group. The group demands absolute loyalty. Anyone who transgresses by not supporting the group or by talking about their activities or plans is completely ostracized. Good times are planned, such as picking and boiling corn in the kitchen to eat after dark, and the ostracized one does not hear about it until afterwards. In large colonies, or among the young people of neighboring colonies, exclusive cliques may develop, but they present a united front to all those who are not in their age set. The adults conveniently "do not see" the mild transgressions, and the young people enjoy the thrill of semiforbidden behavior and of escape from adult surveillance.

The "foolish years" are a time for trying the boundaries. The young person will eventually grow to the point where he will reject the world and choose the colony way of life, but during this time there is some flirtation with the world, some learning about that which will be rejected. Most young people have photographs taken (no one should make a graven image), many have their own cameras. Some boys own small transistor radios on which they listen to Western songs and from which they memorize the songs. Some trap during the winter and sell the furs, or moonlight to earn extra money. Quite a few of the boys own wristwatches, and occasionally boys smoke secretly. The girls have colored nail polish and may use it to paint their toenails, which are hidden under heavy black laced shoes. They have perfume, dime-store jewelry, and sometimes fancy underwear. The in-between years are a period of limited self-realization. In extreme cases a young man may leave the colony for a few weeks, several months, or even for a couple of years. He is a "tourist" in the outside world: he learns about it, earns some money, but always plans to return to the colony to marry and raise his family.

There is a tendency, more pronounced among the girls, to create a secret world. As long as the make-believe does not interfere with the young peoples' work and is not flaunted, adults tacitly accept it and, remembering their own youth, are tolerant. Sometimes the secret world is confined to a locked wooden chest; sometimes a corner of the attic is made into a personal microcosm. Here are stored bits of the temporal world; photographs, sheet music, suntan lotion, and souvenirs. These artifacts represent, however meagerly, what the individual has the freedom to pursue or the freedom to renounce. They represent the world outside the colony; they represent the self in its indulgent, vanity-pleasing aspects. As the individual matures and measures these trinkets and indulgences against the full life of the colony, the young person generally finds the satisfactions received from active participation in the colony far outweigh those of self-development. A Hutterite young person's self-image requires colony identification.

During much of this transitional period, the young person is measuring himself or herself first as a member of the peer group and then as a colony member. The young person generally has a considerable interest in the outside world that eventually helps him to understand better what it means to be a Hutterite. His status within the nuclear family is quite high during this period, before beginning a family of his own. During the last year or so as a young person, he is expected to show by his works, in other words, by his daily behavior, that he can adhere to the rules of the colony. When the individual has displayed by actions, and knows with his heart and mind that he or she cannot continue as an irresponsible child, the young person willingly and humbly requests baptism, so that he may become a true member of the colony. The goal of the Hutterite system of child rearing has then been achieved.

BAPTISM

Hutterite ritual prepares the individual for two important rites of passage. The first is baptism, the second death. Baptism is essential for adult participation in the ritual of daily life; death leads the true Hutterite into life everlasting. There are close parallels between baptism and death. In order to be baptized, the "old man," the natural man, must die so the "spiritual man" may be born; the human body must die in order that the spiritual man may be released into eternal life. Both rites of passage stress death as an essential step to life.

Every Hutterite has a birthright place in the colony that insures his constant care. Should the individual die during childhood before reaching the age of discretion, he or she is assured a place in heaven. When the child is able to differentiate between good and evil, he or she becomes responsible for making the correct choice. The young person requests baptism and, after a period of instruction, is initiated into church membership. He or she retains this membership until death, unless some major transgression of the rules should cause the church to exclude him or her either temporarily or permanently.

Baptism is equated with submission to the church. The applicant must desire "to yield himself to God with all his heart and all his soul and all his members . . . to live no more to himself" (Rideman 1950:79). A present-day Hutterite bishop writes: "He who will not be steadfast with the godly, to suffer the evil as well as the good, and accept all as good, however the Lord may direct, let him remain away. . . . We desire to persuade no man with smooth words. It is not a matter of human compulsion or necessity, for God wants voluntary service" (Hofer 1955:24–25). A seventeen-year-old Hutterite girl said, "Before you ask to be baptized, you know here [pointing to her heart] and here [pointing to her head] that you can't live any longer without it."

Since babyhood, the Hutterite has been socialized to believe that the collective unit is more important than the separate individuals who make up the group. From the time the babies are seven weeks old they have learned to fit into a group pattern, and they have been treated as members of a group rather than as individuals. They first identify with the nuclear family, then with the peer group in school, and finally with the post-school work group. With each successive stage of development, the number of people above the individual decreases and the number below increases. Each Hutterite has been taught to serve and obey those above him and to care for and direct those below him. Within the peer group there is some competition (primarily in work performance), but there is strong support, especially in the face of threat from the outside. Now, when a person requests baptism, the whole colony becomes, in effect, the peer group. From the time they have known what a comb is used for, Hutterite children have been taught to obey. "When children from little up are used to obeying their God-fearing parents," says a Hutterite sermon, "then they will have formed a habit of obeying, and it will be a lot easier for them to obey Jesus Christ."

Girls are about nineteen or twenty, and boys between twenty and twenty-six, when baptized. One preacher explained that even the state does not allow people under twenty-one to vote, and baptism, being a much more important decision than voting, should not be undertaken much before twenty-one and perhaps a little later. Another preacher explained, "Christ was baptized at thirty years of age, and so if someone does not desire this until twenty-five or thirty years of age, we must be patient with such a person. Some people don't seem to understand until they are quite old—but it's not right to make God wait so long." The goal of child rearing among the Hutterites is the individual's voluntary decision to submit himself to the *Gemein*. All the child's life has been, in effect, a preparation for this major rite of passage.

"He who is to be baptized must first request, ask for, and desire it," wrote Rideman in the sixteenth century. In all colonies the individual makes the request to be baptized in a highly stylized form and generally with the support of a peer group. The colony members decide months in advance, often a year or so in advance, that they will have baptism that particular year, and generally it is known by everyone in the colony who is going to request baptism and who will wait. There may be a question about one or two of the candidates, but these too are discussed, so that by the time the young people are ready to submit formal application, the colony is in agreement; quite often a young person is advised not to request baptism yet. The instruction period lasts six to eight weeks, during which time candidates are admonished as a group on Sunday afternoon for about two-and-a-half to three hours. Baptism is held every year in some colonies, but many colonies baptize only once every two to five years. If there is only one person who needs baptism, that individual may be taken to a neighboring colony to join their group of applicants for instruction. Normally, the baptismal service takes place on Palm Sunday but also occasionally at Pentecost.

The Hutterites teach that right belief leads to right behavior. Thus, it is not enough for the young Hutterite to profess belief verbally; he or she must also show in everyday actions the fruit of this belief. His or her behavior in all areas must be acceptable to the church community. There is a greater emphasis on correct acting than on correct thinking. The catechism asks, "What is the inner shame?" The reply is "when a man has sinful thoughts, which he should dispose of." It asks, "What is sin?" The answer is "The transgression of the law." Wrong thinking is bad, but wrong behavior is sin.

The whole colony cooperates in admonishing, punishing, and forgiving its members. During the period of instruction for baptism, the applicants are carefully watched, for they must demonstrate that they have really humbled themselves, are devoid of self-will, and are completely obedient to the community. In the course of instruction in one colony, the applicants formally request baptism thirty-six times. Each must know that he or she really desires and is ready to make the greatest commitment of his or her life.

The baptismal ceremony consists of two parts: Saturday afternoon the candidates are examined about their belief and are asked as many as twenty-five questions; on Sunday afternoon the candidates are baptized. The preacher places his hands on each applicant, while his assistant pours a small quantity of pure water on the head of each. The preacher offers a prayer that they may be preserved in piety and faith until death.

One adolescent Hutterite girl explained, "When you are baptized, then you are really old." The German school mother said of the changes baptism required, "Up until this time, his will was not renounced, now it is; and he's obligated to report anything he sees that is not correct in the colony. He must always speak to such a one before he reports. He has restricted himself." In other words, baptism signifies the voluntary acceptance of responsibility for the actions of everyone in the colony. It signifies the internalization of Hutterite values.

After baptism, men are given voting privileges and are eligible for more responsible work assignments. There is no change in the work status of the girls. Both men and women who have been baptized may attend weddings and funerals in other colonies. It is customary for the newly baptized young people to travel to other colonies. Baptism is assumed to be the first step leading to marriage, for baptism must precede marriage, as one's commitment to God takes precedence over one's commitment to one's spouse. Ideally, the time between baptism and marriage is not long, especially for a young man. It is said that an unmarried man is like a garden that has no fence. "He needs a wife and family to protect him." Defection is less likely to occur after marriage. Often, a young man is not baptized until he is contemplating marriage. A young girl who is seriously interested in a young man may be persuaded to wait to be baptized, and this often has the effect of postponing her marriage for several years.

The baptized but yet unmarried persons are on the fringe of the young people's social life. They participate in the pattern of dating, but have little to do with the testing of the boundaries or the tasting of the world that is characteristic of this age. They have made their choice and have, to a considerable extent, lost interest in the material trinkets of a rejected way of life. They prefer to use their energies to help their colony succeed.

With baptism the relationship between the parents and the child becomes closer. The growing child has become a member of the colony, and the parents treat the young person as a colony member as well as an offspring. They, with the help of God and the colony, have accomplished their task of raising this child "in the nurture and admonition of the Lord," and now that their child has become a part of the *Gemein* they can enjoy the new member. The children have become the spiritual brothers and sisters of their parents, and they can work together almost as peers and can identify more closely with one another. The child remains emotionally dependent, but there is no longer the sharp division between parent and child that existed earlier. Within the hierarchical power structure of the colony, the sons tend to cooperate closely with their father and with their biological brothers, and in a highly integrated colony, these patterns are extended to include all the baptized men of the colony. The daughters continue to identify closely with their peer group of girls. They remain under the direction of their mother and father, who realize that too soon their daughter will marry, probably to a man from another colony, and when she moves to her husband's colony, they will miss her company and her service. In her new home she will be under the direction of her husband, but she will identify most closely with the married women who form her new peer group.

MARRIAGE AND ADULTHOOD

Courtship among the Hutterites is usually long, from about two to six years. There is a great deal of variation in the degree of secretiveness maintained and in the opportunity couples have to visit each other. Some couples are known by everyone to be going together. This is advantageous because they are more likely to be able to visit one another when the truck goes between colonies on business. Other couples may tell no one other than their families until shortly before they hope to be married. Very frequently, more than one couple is married at the same time, sometimes as many as five. Marriages may not take place immediately before Christmas or from the period just before Easter until after Pentecost.

The description of a specific wedding will illustrate the pattern of festivities. The couple had known each other for at least five years, but had only visited one another about five or six times. The bride had never been to the groom's colony. They were informally engaged for six months before the wedding, but the "news was not out" until about two weeks before the groom came to ask for her hand. The young man asked his parents if he could be married; then he asked the first preacher who, in turn, asked the council. He was given the consent of his colony and a letter to the preacher of the girl's colony, stating that he had colony permission for the marriage. The groom arrived at the bride's colony with his father and his grandfather on a Wednesday. They spoke to the first preacher of the bride's colony, who asked the members of the council if they would let her go. In the evening the groom and his father went to the parents of the bride, and the groom's father asked her parents if they would give their daughter to his son. Her parents gave their consent and then asked their daughter if she accepted the young man. She consented and changed to a new dark purple dress, and everyone of church age in the colony proceeded to the church. Here, formal engagement vows were taken. Among other questions, the preacher asked the young man: "Do you desire to go before her in such a way that she finds in you a mirror and an example of honesty and will be led to the Lord through you, so that you may live together as Christians, one being of benefit to the other?" The preacher added, "Marriage has its share of grief and not every day is filled with happiness, but brings suffering too, as the women are the weaker ones." To the young woman is said, "Since God has ordained that the husband is and should be the head of the wife, I ask you: Do you wish to obey him in all right and godly things as it is the duty of the wife, so that you can serve each other in Godliness?" The service lasted approximately fifteen minutes. After the service, the couple returned to the girl's apartment. The suitor took a pitcher of wine and the bride-to-be a tray with eight tiny tumblers, and they served her parents and his father. Then they proceeded to every house, serving the people and receiving good wishes for their married life. Everyone, including the school children, went into the kitchen. The tables had been arranged around the room; the engaged couple sat in the center opposite the door and all the others sat around the edges of the dining room, singing wedding songs and enjoying a lunch. About 10:00 P.M. the children and old folk went to bed, and the young people adjourned to one of the extra rooms in the colony. There, the singing went on until about midnight. Thursday night there was another *hulba* (festivity) in the kitchen. Friday the couple left for the young man's colony. Before they left, all the colony members brought small presents to the bride-to-be: a bedspread, a table lamp, flatware, an alarm clock, an electric steam iron, plates, towels, soap, a small table, a half slip, a bread box, a laundry basket, a wastepaper basket, and pillow cases. In addition, she received from the colony extra cloth for dresses, bedding, and a new electric sewing machine. The colony contributions are not considered to be gifts; they have been earned and are due the engaged girl. Three panel trucks took the girl, her belongings, and her relatives to her fiancé's colony. Even though the father of the groom-to-be had telephoned the householder that a wedding was to be arranged, as soon as the truck arrived, the young people of the colony eagerly opened the doors, inquiring if the young man had been successful in getting his bride. The young girl in question was introduced to the young girls of the colony and everyone went to the kitchen where they were all fed supper and had another evening of singing.

On Sunday morning the wedding took place. The bride wore a dress of blue brocade. Her uncle, who is the first preacher in her colony, had the major part of the service and asked the couple almost exactly the same questions they had been asked at the engagement. After the vows, he blessed them, saying, "We herewith bear witness that you marry each other as God-fearing partners according to the order of God and the example of the forefathers and with the knowledge and counsel of the elders of the whole congregation." After the service there was a wedding meal complete with wedding cake, followed by more singing and another snack. Everyone was given a bag of nuts and sweets to take home. After supper one wedding song was sung. The bridal couple visited with the guests during the evening and finally returned to their own room.

Everyone in the colony looks forward to a wedding. It is the happiest gathering of relatives and friends. Former acquaintances can be renewed, relatives can visit with one another, and young people can court. A wedding is a lot of work for the colony and quite an expense. This is one of the reasons given for encouraging double or triple weddings. But it is also because the brides and grooms enjoy a joint wedding and like to do things in groups. The more couples being married, the more guests will be present and the bigger and more festive the crowd. Weddings function to formalize marriage, to make explicit the relationship of the two colonies involved, to bring relatives together, and to strengthen intercolony ties by pleasant visitation. In the socialization of the individual the wedding is a rite of passage to a new stage of life. In contrast to the long, rigorous preparation for baptism, the preparation for marriage is incidental. The adjustment for the groom is minimized. Often he retains his former room in or adjoining his parents' apartment. His brothers move out and his bride moves in. There is no change in his pattern of work, except that he becomes eligible for a more responsible position.

For the bride, marriage involves a tremendous adjustment. Generally she moves into a new colony, sometimes a colony she has never visited. She leaves her parents, her siblings, and her peer group. Her work patterns change, both because she is now married, but also because she is in a different colony where things are done slightly different. She is, however, given a niche, for the bedroom is referred to as her room, not their room or his room. The bedroom belongs to the wife and mother, the colony to the husband. She is under the direction of her mother-in-law. The husband is in an emotionally strong position. All his primary ties are maintained and, in addition, he has a wife. Every detail of the colony is familiar to him. He knows a great deal about all aspects of the colony and about every member of the colony. In contrast, his wife is in a vulnerable position. She has only her husband to turn to for support and information. The marriage patterns function to support the husband in his dominant position and to emphasize the dependence of the wife.

Education for pregnancy and childbirth is even more rudimentary than formal preparation for marriage. Pregnancy and childbirth are not discussed in the presence of girls. Daughters are generally living in another colony when they become pregnant,

Newlyweds

and their mothers do not come to care for them until after the baby has been born. There is little recognition of pregnancy, no change in work schedule, no special knowledge that is imparted to the gravid woman. Most young women have been told practically nothing about the details of labor. However, the girls have grown up in a society with a high birth rate and a positive attitude towards babies. They have been taught to ignore discomfort and to accept without complaint whatever is to be their lot. The attitude toward pregnancy and childbirth appears to be one of passive acceptance, or when there are already many children, of mild annoyance. In contrast, the attitude toward the delivered baby is one of positive enjoyment.

Constant reinforcement is necessary for the adult person. The Sunday and daily services are part of the continuous formal socialization of the individual. These group ceremonials have both the functions of teaching the young and of reinforcing the beliefs the adults have internalized. All adults must set a good example at all times. In virtually all activities, adult Hutterites function within the age-set hierarchy and participates primarily in same-sex groups. On the job both the adult man and woman are constantly participating in decision making that must follow a pattern, enabling the group to reach consensus. One individual does not persuade the group or put forward arguments; rather a subject is discussed in such a way that most of the individuals have participated and the final decision is indeed a group decision. The very youngest adult men may still be in hard labor positions, those older are in leadership positions such as departmental heads of various economic enterprises, while the oldest men tend to be in executive positions, that is, on the council. Although there may be muted competition within the group for various positions, and fairly obvious competition among the different positions to demonstrate how efficiently an operation can be run, the general pattern is for the individual to progress to higher status positions as he grows older.

Within the well-integrated colony there are no contests for place (place is determined by age and sex) or for office (office is determined by vote of the *Gemein*). Hutterites do not feel comfortable with the satisfaction that might come from a position of dominance. They have been well socialized against self-assertion. "One must not take upon himself" but must "wait until God chooseth" (Rideman 1950:80). Power, authority, and influence are diffused among the mature men and expressed as group action. Biological brothers cooperate closely among themselves and with their father in all areas of life, but this is not necessarily disruptive to the colony as a whole. These men have learned to handle their emotions of jealousy and competition and to work smoothly together, counting on one another's strengths and compensating for one another's weaknesses. The early identification and constant interaction with the peer group have taught the men to work well with those who will be their spiritual brothers. One's spiritual brother is in no sense an outsider or an "other." One's emotions towards him are somewhat less intense than towards one's biological brother, and therefore easier to control. In making colony decisions, brother groups are functional. News spreads informally among biological brothers, and among themselves they argue noisily and freely the relative merits of various alternatives. Quite often, consensus is reached within one family of brothers. When members of one set of brothers interact with members of another, the problem can be further discussed, with each individual knowing that he has some support. Often a decision can be reached fairly quickly. The men have been socialized against stubbornness, and have been taught that when a colony issue reaches the voting stage, the church members must vote as spiritual brothers rather than as biological brothers. Biological brothers function as a closely cooperating subgroup within the larger cooperative. Women do not vote and have limited influence on colony decision making. However, in those areas directly affecting them, the women cooperate closely, applying unified pressure on their husbands and adult sons, who eventually reach consensus supporting the women's request.

Social controls are based primarily on the individual's fear of rejection. The adult Hutterite has identified with the group, and for his own self-esteem needs full acceptance by the group. Even an indication of possible rejection is threatening. The simplest form of social control is admonishment by a member of the peer group. If there is a misunderstanding between individuals, it is their responsibility to straighten it out. If one person is troubled about the conduct of another, he or she should go and speak to that person. If this is of no avail, the preacher will speak privately to the erring member. Should the transgressor still not desist, the erring individual may be spoken to privately by one or more members, or may be asked to come before the council and the *Gemein*. If it is a problem that involves a large proportion of the baptized men, such as drinking, several outside preachers may be asked to step in and help. The preachers obtain all the pertinent facts, admonish the offenders in the presence of all baptized men, and then call on them to repent and seal the repentance by each man shaking hands with every other man. There are various degrees of formal punishment for different transgressions. "Pardon" is the least stringent form of punishment for the baptized person. The offender must stand in church after the sermon and confess his fault to the church for "whatsoever she [the Church] forgiveth is forgiven here and in eternity" (Rideman 1950:44). "Discord" is an offense demanding more serious punishment for the baptized member. The offender may be guilty of instigating quarrels or fomenting disunity in the group. He or she is severed (banned) from church membership temporarily, for a few days or a week, during which time the banned person may not shake hands or eat with other members but must eat alone, usually after the adult meal. Because Hutterites believe that a person who dies outside the church must spend eternity burning in hell and that his or her life has been wasted, they take great pains to protect the vulnerable person from any physical danger and from accidental death. The erring member is believed to be repentant when he or she shows it in his or her attitude and behavior, when "one senseth that the Lord hath again drawn nigh to him, been gracious to and accepted him" (Rideman 1950:133). Should an offender continue in waywardness, as in the case of persistent drunkenness or practicing a heretical religious doctrine, the ban may continue indefinitely. Some of these persons eventually leave the colony. Other than the shedding of blood, which the church cannot forgive, the worst possible offense is desertion of the colony. The members entertain no hope of heaven for anyone who dies outside the church.

A successfully socialized adult Hutterite gets along well with others, is cheerful, and has a kind word for everyone. He is submissive and obedient to the rules and regulations of the colony. He is a hard, responsible worker. A woman may be praised by the statement, "She is always first in the kitchen when the work bell rings." An adult Hutterite must never display anger or hostility or precipitate quarrels. Intensity and imagination are not admired; rather, a quiet willingness coupled with hard work are held in high esteem. The constant pruning that adapts each individual to the group leads to a minimizing of differences and the muting of emotional expression. The subduing of individuality is implied in the Hutterite saying, "No man with rights has a right to all of his rights." The elimination of extremes and the imposition of a strict order enable the members to find satisfaction in the "narrow way" that leads to salvation.

Hutterites view themselves as having many friends, both inside and outside of the colonies. Their enemies are those who have persecuted them in the distant past. Hutterites are somewhat more extroverted than introverted on the Myers-Briggs personality indicator. They are sensing rather than intuitive, feeling rather than thinking, and judgmental rather than perceptive. The standard description for the ESFJ type reads:

Warm-hearted, talkative, popular, conscientious, born cooperators, active committee members. Need harmony and may be good at creating it. Always doing something nice for someone. Work best with encouragement and praise. Main interests is in things that directly and visibly affect people's lives. (Myers 1993:7)

AGING

Hutterites age early. A man of forty said, "We older people let the young do the hard work. A seventy-year-old person is considered to be extremely old. Such a person looks old and acts old. The formal aspect of the culture requires that the aged be respected by all younger persons. There is no inducement to act younger than one's age. The pressure to move upward in the age set is invariably present from kindergarten through the last rite of passage, death. Older people are believed to deserve "rest." In such capacity, they may spend more time traveling, going to town, talking with neighbors and visitors; work is optional.

There is no abrupt age of retirement. Women usually are relieved of their rotating colony jobs between the ages of forty-five and fifty. Those who hold the positions of head cook or kindergarten mother continue until they are too old to fulfill these responsibilities. Often women are not assigned to the kindergarten until they are in their forties. The first jobs women give up are milking and hoeing. Milking requires early rising and lifting heavy pails. Usually, they also give up cooking and baking. If they still enjoy these activities, there is opportunity to help a daughter or a daughter-in-law, or to substitute for someone. Most women help with food preparation as long as they are able, for they prefer working to sitting alone in their apartment. When an older person loses a spouse, he or she often moves in with one of the children or into a room adjacent to their apartment. A grandchild is assigned to run errands or even to sleep with the older person during the night. When they become too old or weak to go to the dining room, meals are carried to the rooms of the elderly. Older women who are doing very little colony work will help look after the babies who are brought to their apartment.

Retirement among men is more difficult to manage than among women. The problem is to persuade an older man to give up his position if he wants to keep it. An elderly man is frequently removed from a foreman position and is simultaneously elected to a position on the council if he is not already on the council. In this way, his conservative influence is constructive and the economic development that requires constant change is put into the hands of a younger, more adventurous man. Once elected to the colony council, a man virtually always remains on the council. When a preacher begins to hesitate or forget his long prayer, it is recognized that he must give up some of his responsibility. Often the most difficult person to relieve is the householder. For although conservatism may be an advantage in a preacher, it is a disadvantage in the householder; the colony must be willing to risk capital and remain dynamic in its economic practices. Several years may be required to change householders. Gentle persuasion, rather than coercive measures, is the rule.

Older people who are ill go to physicians in nearby towns. Good health is important to the Hutterites, but medical practices are influenced by the world view that the body is important only insofar as it houses the eternal soul. Hutterites go to accredited physicians near their colonies, and often go to great lengths and expense to obtain special treatment for chronically ill members. The best physicians, usually from large urban centers, are often unavailable to them on account of the great distances involved. Their rather famed sixteenth-century tradition of healing, curing baths, and surgery (Friedman 1961:126) has been greatly altered, but their own contemporary practitioners include midwives, masseurs, bone-setters, and dentists. Physicians who see Hutterite patients report that headaches, constipation, and a variety of neurotic difficulties constitute the major complaints. In an intensive study of their mental health, Eaton and Weil (1955) concluded that the group was well poised and extraordinarily free from the symptoms of mental illness, in spite of disease patterns that were influenced by the culture. The chances of recovery from mental illness, including an affliction known as *Anfechtung* (a state of deep depression and doubt) are excellent (Kaplan and Plaut 1956:67). The disposition to use herbs and teas, as well as the disposition to practice modern preventive medicine, varies greatly along family lines. Poor health is disruptive when it prevents a person from performing his work. Women, especially, entertain fears of losing their health, for with the loss of ability to work there is a loss of status. A sick person, unless he is old, is not given much personal attention and often must take care of himself.

Old people constitute a small minority of the population of any colony because of the large number of children found in all colonies. The aged are not segregated but live with their closest kin. Of a total Hutterite population of 8,542 in 1950, only twenty-five persons were seventy-five or over (Eaton and Mayer 1954:9). Life expectancy is believed to be not strikingly different from the United States population, except that until recently men tended to live longer than women. By 1971 Hutterite women were outliving men (Ingoldsby and Stenton 1988). The psychology of aging and preparation for death is unique and consistent with the culture. Old people are not forced to exert themselves, nor are they denied active participation. Older men can reduce their work load without fear of losing status or of being excluded from the policy-forming group, the *Gemein.* The contribution of an old man to the colony is limited economically, but his strong identity with the tradition of the colony and the respect he gets from young members is a stabilizing influence. The older women, under the veto power of the preacher and the boss, choose the cloth to be purchased for colony use, exerting a conservative influence. They knit socks for their many descendants and watch babies for limited periods of time while the mothers are at meals or doing colony work. Communication between old and young is maintained, and old persons can keep abreast of the changing times as much as they wish. Old age is not a period of loneliness and isolation or of economic deprivation. Occasionally, the oldest active man cuts the fresh loaves of bread and keeps every table in the communal dining hall supplied with bread. He is given the honorable position of *Brotschneider* (bread cutter). He may eat later with the head cook and the householder. In this capacity, the father-figure as provider is symbolically activated in the life of the community.

DEATH

Death to the Hutterites is the termination of the earthly struggle and the beginning of paradise for those who have lived faithfully. In expectation of heaven, all of life has been preparation for death. Life span, from beginning to ending, is determined by God. The time of death is believed to be controlled only by God. After the assassination of President John F. Kennedy, one Hutterite informant said, "His time was up, and no matter where he would have been, up in an airplane or down on the ground, God called his number and he had to go." A basic attitude is expressed in a Hutterite proverb: "When a person comes to his end, great faith is more important than great possessions."

One day the women were discussing a tragedy that occurred to a neighbor's boy. The lad darted in front of the school bus and was killed instantly. "Do you think the boy was just trying to get it over with before he grew up?" asked one. "No. I believe his number was called and he had to die," said another. "It's not so bad when a child dies like that, but we don't like to see a grownup die so suddenly. We prefer slow deaths, not sudden deaths. The people who want to die suddenly are the outsiders," said a preacher. "They want death to be unexpected so that they do not need to think about it, for they don't want to face the future. We prefer a slow death, even if it involves pain, so that we are sure to have plenty of time to consider eternity and to confess and make everything right."

Children who die in their innocence are envied by adults. They are presumed to be innocent, and are thus spared the temptations and the life-long struggles of self-denial. One day little Matilda was playing near a canal and fell into the water. Her older brother rescued her and brought her home, a distance of about one-half mile, on the two-wheeled play cart. She shivered with cold, developed a fever the following day, and pneumonia was predicted. Commenting on the mishap, the preacher said, "If Matilda would have drowned, she surely would have been an angel." An older man said, "When these little ones die we know they are in heaven, but we never know what will happen to them if they grow up. I sure wish I would have died when I was a kid."

The deathbed account of a seventy-five-year-old grandmother, written by one of her children says:

> In her last years our mother occupied herself with knitting and sewing. Her songbook was always open and she learned many lovely songs and verses by heart. Her spirit was directed heavenward and her spirit was quickened through these songs. Her final sickness lasted four weeks and during this time she was examined concerning her life and her goals. All this time she had great difficulty breathing and sleeping and was always conscious and, like the apostle Paul, wanted to go home to be with Christ. She did not wish to recover in this world because her inner pilgrimage had already begun. She looked to her heavenly abode, to which she had already sent many prayers and lovely songs. At her last she told us: "Children, I tell you, live godly, work hard, be faithful, and share with the poor." When she had almost passed on, she asked once more to get up. She stood up straight and then sank into her bed. There she lay, weary and tired of the world. She called her sister to her once more and said, "All, all is finished."

In another deathbed account, a father dying of cancer awoke and began to laugh loudly in the presence of many people (Eaton 1964:94). Asked why he was laughing, he explained that he saw "the heavenly pleasure." He said that he saw his father, his father-in-law, and other departed relatives. When asked how they were dressed, he explained: "All alike, one like the other." He made this comparison: "Take the balls of a ball bearing; they all look the same and, believe me, that is the nicest of it all."

The emotional acceptance of death is supported by many aspects of the culture, specifically by the lack of sentiment attached to property and by adequate provision for all the survivors. Terminal illnesses, rather than sudden or accidental deaths, permit the individual to confess any wrongs, to admonish the children, and to gather the family and close friends, even from distant colonies, about the dying person. The family and the colony is supportive in time of death. Funerals are extremely important occasions, for they permit integration of the society on all levels. Relatives and friends from distant colonies participate in the religious and burial services. Funeral festivities also permit young people to make new friends and look for a prospective mate.

Individuality, which is denied and carefully guarded against throughout life, is completely abolished in the heaven envisioned by the Hutterites. There is little speculation about heaven or the kinds of enjoyment or activity anticipated. What matters most is preparation. There is to be more perfect communal living in heaven. The communal emphasis is inculcated through vigorous teaching from a young age and is reinforced in the visions of the dying. The beliefs and practices so consistently taught during life provide meaning for the members, so that in the final rite of passage there is fulfillment.

5 / The Challenge of Change and Disruption

Insight into a culture is gained not only by observing the society when the culture is highly integrated, but also by observing the culture when there are various threats and unusual problems such as war and population decline. In this chapter the major disruptive patterns in Hutterite society, both internal and external, will be described. Important external threats in their history have been war, hostile outsiders, land and production restrictions, and, to a lesser degree, the public school. Internal threats have been extreme poverty, prosperity, and disruptive converts who join the Hutterites and later leave the faith, taking sympathizers with them.

WAR AND NONRESISTANCE

The Hutterites are a nonresistant people. Their basic beliefs prevent them from retaliation and from taking human life, citing such passages from the teaching of Jesus as "resist not evil," or "do good to those who hate you."

War and its hardships have on several occasions almost extinguished the Hutterites. In their world view Hutterites are not opposed to governments, and their leaders often say, "A poor government is better than none at all." Hutterites respect order and discipline in governments or in the military. For them, as with all Anabaptists, government is believed to be necessary for regulating the carnal order. Christians, they say, should obey government in all matters that do not violate biblical teaching, but should not involve themselves in the administration of government or holding public office. "Christ refused to defend himself and set an example for his followers." The Old Testament law of retribution was repealed, and for the Hutterites warfare must come to an end with the establishment of the true church of Christ. The nature of Hutterite conflict with government has varied with the particular issue in question and the circumstances. Their European experience contrasts sharply with that in North America.

Their early period of prosperity in Moravia ended in 1593 when Turkey and Austria went to war (Friedmann 1961). Soldiers were billeted in the colonies and possessions and livestock were taken. When the Turks invaded Moravia in 1605 they destroyed sixteen colonies and carried away several hundred captives. The Thirty Years' War came in 1618, ending in dire consequences for all of Europe. Moravia joined the Protestant cause, only to be invaded by the Hapsburg army in 1619, which destroyed many colonies. By 1620 the Roman Catholic forces suppressed all other religions in the Hapsburg empire. In 1660 Hutterite colonies in Moravia were plundered by the

Spaniards, Neapolitans, French, Poles, Walloons, Croats, Hungarians, German mus-
keteers, and Saxon calvary (Hutterian Brethren 1987: 654, 658). Men were brutally
tortured and killed; women, girls, and young boys were raped. Many, "mostly sisters," were carried off along with horses, cows, and oxen. Finally, the last of the
twenty-four Moravian colonies was abandoned.

The remaining devout Hutterites who did not accept Catholicism escaped to
Slovakia and located there in fifteen colonies, which survived until 1760. Life in Slovakia was hard and the Jesuits, with encouragement from Maria Theresa, succeeded
in confiscating Hutterite literature and in converting members and baptizing their in-
fants into the Catholic church. Those who turned Catholic for several generations secretly adhered to the communal faith and practice. With forced conversion in
Slovakia, a small group of nineteen persons became the thread to survival. A group
of fifty-six Lutheran refugees joined the remnant of nineteen remaining Hutterites in
1756 in the small country of Transylvania. Just as the Hutterite children were about
to be placed in a Catholic orphanage, the group fled by night to Wallachia. Here they
were soon caught up in a war between Russia and Turkey.

An appeal to a Russian general led to an invitation to settle in the Ukraine. They
were granted religious freedom and liberal terms of settlement, in line with the policies of Catherine the Great toward other German immigrants. A hundred years later,
when conscription was enacted, they migrated to the United States. Thus, in Europe,
the external pressures of war, plunder, coercion, or forced colonization were direct
and disruptive. Only by successive appeals to governments more sympathetic than
their own were they able to survive. A remnant remained loyal to the core of their
faith. The chronicle of the early period (Wolkan 1923), still well-preserved in a contemporary colony, contains a list of 2,175 persons who died a martyr's death during
this extended period. (See also Hutterite Brethren (1987): 217–226.)

In America, war and the fear of conscription scattered the original settlements in
South Dakota to other states and to the provinces of Canada. With the outbreak of the
Spanish-American War, the *Darius-Leut* sought to move to Canada to escape possible military conscription. The privileges asked of the Canadian government were
granted in 1899. One colony moved to Canada but later returned because of poor
farming conditions.

The first Hutterite confrontation with conscription in North America occurred
during World War I. As American patriotism swept the country, and the midwestern
states in particular, the Hutterites suffered harassment from their neighbors. Many
Americans thought they were pro-German and therefore enemies. Young Hutterites
were drafted and ordered to report for army duty. They refused army service and
were segregated in army barracks and guard houses. The law made no provision for
sincere conscientious objectors. Hutterite leaders sent a special appeal to President
Woodrow Wilson. Three Hutterite representatives went to Washington to seek clari-
fication of a law that provided for noncombatant service for religious objectors under
terms to be prescribed by the president, and to obtain permission for their young men
to move with the colonies to Canada. They met with little success because Secretary
of War Newton Baker could not be located. Meanwhile, young men were being
court-martialed and placed in barracks and ridiculed at home. The colonies were hu-
miliated and persecuted by unsympathetic neighbors. They would "capture" a young

man and forcibly cut his beard into ridiculous shapes. The Hutterites were accused by outsiders of smuggling glass into their own flour mills and then were accused of sabotage. The State Council of Defense set as its goal the elimination of all pro-Germanism, prohibiting the use of the German language in public or in churches. The newspapers charged the Hutterites with making wartime profits and with lack of patriotism. Although Hutterites were willing to give money for relief and offered $10,000 for this purpose, they refused to buy war bonds. A group of patriots visited the Jamesville colony, and without opposition, drove to market a hundred steers and a thousand sheep to force the colony to buy bonds. The packing houses refused to touch the stolen cattle. They were sold for $14,000, or about half their true value. The money was refused by the National War Loan Committee and was subsequently deposited in a local bank in the name of Hutterites. The Hutterites refused to accept the money. (Later, it was accepted by a Canadian land agent as a down payment on land.) The colonies experienced raids from local citizens, who confiscated their wine under the Prohibition Act but drank it at the county seat. The ridicule and torture of four drafted men—Jacob Wipf and three Hofer brothers, Joseph, David, and Michael—was one of the most shocking incidents to come out of this country's experience with conscientious objectors (see pages 9–10). The cruel treatment and deaths of Joseph and Michael Hofer seemed to the Hutterites like a return to the sixteenth century. All of these events culminated in a mass migration to Canada beginning in 1918.

The move to Canada did not proceed without difficulties concerning Canadian immigration laws, the sale of land at sacrificial prices, and a final legal suit brought by the state of South Dakota. The State Council of Defense had stipulated that 5 percent of the sale price of Hutterite land be invested in war bonds and that one-half percent be given to the Red Cross. The Hutterites resolved this problem by lowering the selling price by this amount and letting the buyers purchase the bonds. In a final move against the Hutterites, the State Council of Defense persuaded the state attorney general to use legal action to revoke the articles of incorporation of all Hutterite colonies. The contestants in the trial claimed that the Hutterites had amassed a fortune of over a million dollars in assets and "had dedicated none of it to the worship of God according to any religious belief, for they did not even have a church building" (Conkin 1964:62). It was argued that the corporation had abused its articles of incorporation in unauthorized business activities unrelated to religion, and on this basis the state court asked that it dispose of all land and secular assets within ninety days. Noncompliance meant that the corporation would be declared bankrupt and all assets would be seized. Those who advanced the suit described the Hutterites as a menace to society. They resented their use of the German language, the control of the colony over the children, and their restrictions against mingling with outsiders. On the basis of the suit, the State Council of Defense invited individual Hutterites to leave the colonies and to claim their share of colony property. Not a single individual took advantage of the invitation.

With the outbreak of World War II, there were fifty-two colonies in all of North America. Only six colonies were left in the United States, in spite of the efforts of local governments to attract the Hutterites back during the financial depression of the '30s. One colony was in Montana and five were in South Dakota. In both the

United States and Canada there was a more tolerant attitude and greater facility for dealing with conscientious objectors than during World War I. The Selective Service Act in the United States provided for the assignment of conscientious objectors to civilian public service workcamps. The cost of the camps was underwritten by various religious groups. Hutterite draftees were assigned to these camps, and the colonies contributed toward the cost of maintenance. Conscientious objectors in Canada were assigned to forestry service. Colonies were required to contribute monthly assessments to the Red Cross for each youth drafted. Many were deferred for farm work. A few Hutterites chose jail. There was a total of 276 Hutterites in both countries who served in workcamps for objectors, and 26 who joined the armed forces. After World War II, young Hutterite men in the United States who were drafted served as conscientious objectors and were assigned to work in national parks. They receive a maintenance allowance from the government for their living expenses and continued to live communally in a separate house during the two years of government service.

Throughout their history, war has been a significant external force on Hutterite society. In earlier times the society was in danger of complete extinction by genocide and forced assimilation. In more modern days wars have produced migration and have intensified the cleavages between the colonies and the "world." The twentieth-century treatment of the Hutterites is but a subtle continuation of the persecutions that were so widespread in the sixteenth century. The direct hostility of the sixteenth century has been displaced by more humane considerations and a tendency for the dominant society to use more sophisticated (legal) means of expressing intolerance. But to the Hutterite, the modern forms of persecution have a more sinister connotation than the cruel persecution faced by the founding fathers. Renewed intolerances are a constant reminder to the Hutterites that they are completely dependent upon God for their security.

NEIGHBORING PRACTICES

The colonies vary in their public relations practices. The formal pattern forbids certain kinds of associations with non-Hutterites, which, as stated in the chapter on world view, is based upon the doctrine of separation from the world. Of the several colonies studied intensively and of a great many observed, it was found that the most self-sufficient colony tended to display the most conspicuous ethnocentric patterns and had the poorest public relations. The colony with the smallest number of people and the most geographically isolated deliberately cultivated favorable neighborly relations. One colony that is widely reputed for its progressive agricultural practices permits visitors regularly by appointment. After a tour of the grounds, lunch is served and the visitors are seated in the church for a "lecture" by the preacher, with a discussion period following.

Attitudes toward the Hutterites prior to their moving into a new area are often very different from those that prevail once a colony is established (Serl 1964:111–129). In addition to the fears expressed that a colony would not contribute to the local economy and that land prices would soar upward, there is an element of vexation caused by the Hutterite refusal to mix socially in the local community. Contrary to the fear of local representatives concerned with the economy, Hutterite colonies do make substantial economic contributions to the community, as has been observed in Saskatchewan by Bennett (1967) and in Manitoba by Ryan (1977). In one small, new colony in an area where there are no other colonies nearby, formal neighboring relations are excellent. Neighboring farmers come to the colony for specialized tractor-repair services, to get their seeds cleaned in colony plants, and to get machines for spraying their crops. These services, often with additional assistance in planting and haying for neighbors, are more a gesture toward cultivating good neighborly relations than a desired source of colony income. "We have to be accommodating, and we will not turn anybody away," said the colony preacher. The same colony also loaned a young man as a tractor operator to the municipal road-building crew for a few weeks.

The large colony, which is often self-sufficient and less sensitive to maintaining good public relations, views its informal relations with neighbors differently. The predicament was well stated by one colony spokesman:

> We have a number of neighbors with whom we exchange work and machinery. The more contact we have with neighbors, the more chance our boys have to buddy up with them. We don't mind favoring them with help, but then they want to favor our boys by taking them into their homes, letting them listen to the radio, television, taking them to shows, and then our colony rules are broken. When we tell our neighbors not to do this, they just get mad, and then there is friction.

Hostile acts from outsiders are taken for granted and are built into the world view. When acts of hostility do occur, they tend to function as a cohesive force, thereby integrating the structural relations of the society. When there is no "persecution" or anti-Hutterite sentiment, Hutterite leaders acknowledge a tendency toward internal disruptive patterns. While publicity is not shunned, favorable articles about them are disturbing to some of the more sensitive leaders, who say: "We don't like horn tooting. It makes people jealous, and creates hard feelings." Writers and reporters who visit colonies and hear individuals unburden their grievances often assume naively that relations can be helped by the right kind of publicity. Additional knowledge about Hutterites does not necessarily assure a more tolerant attitude on the part of neighbors (Priestly 1959). Vandalism from unsympathetic gangs is unpredictable and harassing to colonies. "The town people often call to tell us to come and get our geese which are roaming the streets," said a Hutterite woman. "We know who the teen-age boys are that let them loose but their parents don't care and the police do nothing about it." Other intrusions range from broken windows, pilfering tools and supplies, to armed robbery. Cattle thievery occurs in some of the sparsely populated areas of the prairie country. One colony suffered the loss of thirty head of fattened hogs. Pranks such as putting harmful substances into gasoline tanks are disruptive and costly. Some colonies are summoned by telephone in case of fire in nearby small towns; they help willingly. Once when a false alarm was sprung on the colony, a Hutterite told a local official:

> Don't depend on us anymore in case of fire. The last time a call came at midnight, and the snow and mud was as deep as our butts. We got our trucks and tractors out, spent the

whole night until 8:00 in the morning trying to get our vehicles home. Some fool pulled a false alarm.

Hutterite segregation is perhaps one of the most intolerable vices, as viewed by the larger society. The many symbolic ways in which Hutterites isolate themselves gives rise to a variety of myths and falsehoods about their communal life. These falsifications eventually are harmful because of the misinformation provided to the public via mass media. In spite of these distortions, the persecution and dislikes expressed by outsiders tend to strengthen the internal cohesion of the colony.

Individual acts and habits, like not leaving a tip in the restaurant or refusing to lead a prayer at a village gathering, do not trouble the conscience of the individual Hutterite. The individual Hutterite involved may not realize that although his own reputation is not at stake, there is frequently a negative reflection on the colony as a whole.

LEGAL RESTRICTIONS

The growth of Hutterite population is anything but static. Colonies continue to branch out, and new colonies are in the process of being built. During the past three decades (1963–1994), the average colony size has declined slightly, from 94 to 88 persons, and the total population has increased from about 14,000 to 35,000. Their geographic area has expanded. Today, there are five colonies in the state of Washington, five in North Dakota, four in Minnesota, and one in British Columbia. In addition to spreading into new states and provinces, the colonies have moved farther north. The short growing season has necessitated changes in agriculture. Although communal in their lifestyle, Hutterites function as a corporation in their financial contacts with outside society. They are bound by laws and government regulations. They are also governed by the marketplace. There is considerable variation among the *Leut* as they move into specialized agriculture and small manufacturing businesses. In Canada, government quotas have been a problem, leading colonies to purchase noncontiguous land in order to obtain quotas.

Most of the adverse sentiments against Hutterites can be grouped into three categories: dislike of their separatism, charges of unfair economic competition, and fear of unprecedented growth. As long as these negative sentiments operate informally, they present no major threat to the colonies. When they are formalized into laws, they disrupt the expansion patterns of the colonies. Alberta passed a law in 1942 that prevented the sale of land to enemy aliens and Hutterites. In 1947 the colonies were permitted to buy up to 6,400 acres of land for each new colony if the site was forty miles from an existing colony. The law was changed in 1960 by eliminating the forty-mile clause and requiring hearings before a community property control board and approval by the legislative cabinet. The board had to recommend in each instance "whether or not it is in the public interest to permit the sale of land." Since these laws have been in effect, colonies have tended to expand northward in Alberta and to locate in Montana (since 1948) or Saskatchewan (since 1952), and in Washington (since 1960). In 1972 the Communal Properties Act became inoperative.

This colony changed its source of economic productivity from agriculture to manufacturing.

When the Alberta colonies branched into Saskatchewan, there was immediate local opposition. The provincial government conducted a survey (Canadian Mental Health Association, 1953) to explore the nature and extent of the problem and concluded that the colonies presented no threat and that future clashes could be alleviated by disseminating proper information. A Provincial Committee on Minority Groups established a liaison officer to anticipate and assist in a settlement program which would free communities from the fear of being overrun by the colonies.

There was agitation in Manitoba to introduce legislation to restrict the colonies, but a legislative committee urged that no restrictions be placed on "the fundamental right" to purchase land. All attempts at restrictive laws in Manitoba have failed, but in 1954 the Union of Manitoba Municipalities demanded restrictions on the acreage and location of colonies. This culminated in an agreement in which the Hutterites consented to locate no more than two colonies in large municipalities and one colony in small ones, to limit new colony acreage to 5,120 acres, and to keep colonies at least ten miles apart. The threat of legislation affected the land-buying pattern of the colonies, in some instances long before any formal agreements were reached. Some colonies in Manitoba responded to the threat of legislation by establishing daughter colonies in South Dakota.

The effect of Canadian land restrictions on the colonies has been a dispersion of their settlements into wider geographic areas. The older colonies are unaffected, except for limitations on additional land purchases. Another effect has been the formalization of the three *Leut* into a single legal entity. With the suggestion and assistance of legal advisors, a charter was granted to the Hutterite colonies of Canada by the Canadian Parliament in 1951. Each *Leut* is defined as a church conference and elects three members to a nine-member board of directors of the Hutterite Brethren Church. The board elects a chairman or senior elder and meets annually, usually with a legal representative. The formal organization allows more unified representation to government, encourages discussion and prediction of problems among the colonies, and encourages greater consensus among the *Leut.* This Canadian charter specifies that property rights belong to the individual colonies, and that disciplinary functions are the prerogative of each *Leut.* The charter protects the colonies against individual members who might desert the colony and make a claim to the corporate property. The constitution was amended and reinstated following a division among the *Schmied-Leut* in 1993. The division was precipitated by the lack of confidence in Elder Jacob Kleinsasser, who was confronted with twelve grievances. By majority vote he was removed as elder of the Hutterian Brethren Church. The amended constitution prevents a senior elder of a *Leut* (conference) from serving as president of the church. This amendment was designed to prevent one person from assuming too much power.

After very severe measures to dissolve the colonies during World War I, South Dakota encouraged the colonies to return during the years of the Depression. Pacifism was a remote issue, the state needed tax revenues, and local governments needed occupants for deserted farm lands. A law was passed in 1935, enabling the colonies to incorporate with the same tax privileges granted to cooperatives. While they would have to pay local taxes, there would be no state and federal corporate taxes. Many of the colonies returned. But faced with bitter opposition to the colonies, the South Dakota legislature passed a bill in 1955 intended to curb Hutterite expansion. It prohibited expansion by any of the incorporated colonies (fifteen in all) from the purchase or lease of land. The bill did not prevent new colonies from forming. Efforts to introduce restrictive laws in Montana and Minnesota have to date not succeeded.

Individual colonies each face their own local and often very peculiar legal tangles. Although the leaders are adept in cultivating friendships with influential outsiders and in arguing on a practical level, they are also trapped into exorbitant prices and leases that require legal counsel. Virtually all colonies have a legal advisor. The several suits brought by defecting members against colony corporations to obtain a share of the communal assets have all failed. The promise not to lay claim to the colony property is written into the baptismal vow, as well as in the articles of incorporation.

The popular impression that Hutterites would purchase unlimited acres of land to add to their present holdings if they could, and that they would exercise no voluntary restraints on either the location or pattern of settlement, is not true. That they will eventually outnumber the rural farm population, a fear expressed by some farm organizations, has no empirical basis. The colonies in Alberta own or lease on the average about 7,200 acres per colony, less than 1 percent of the agricultural lands in the province. The average number of acres owned per person in colonies is 58, while land acreage per person among farm families in Alberta counties where Hutterites live is about 122. Lands owned and operated by South Dakota colonies average 4,640 acres per colony (Riley and Priestly 1959). The farm population displaced by new colonies varies with the area but is usually minimal. One colony of sixty-five persons acquired 6,000 acres of land, and the total population displaced was only six persons. The farms acquired are frequently operated by absentee owners or by aged farmers who wish to retire. Studies of the spending habits of the colonies in comparison with farm families show distinct differences (Bennett 1967). Hutterites spend less per capita for consumer goods than do individual farmers, but the influx of colony population into the area requires expenditures of an amount no less than that spent by the displaced population. The colony consumes large amounts of building supplies and farm equipment.

Discrimination against the Hutterites has diminished during the past thirty years, particularly among small farmers, who know that they cannot compete with the Hutterite system. Another factor responsible for lessening the prejudice against them was the passage of the Canadian Bill of Rights in 1972. This bill repealed Alberta's Communal Property Act of 1942.

The Hutterites are pacifist and refuse to serve in the military; they are committed to "nonresistance" as a way of life. When conflict arises, they will seek peaceful ways to resolve the differences. If that is not possible, they will employ lawyers to defend their rights against challenges. When a municipal district in rural Saskatchewan initiated a zoning code to prohibit domestic dwellings of more than two households per quarter-section of land, the Hutterite colony brought suit. Lawyers for the Hutterites demonstrated that the ordinance was designed to discriminate against the Hutterites, who were seeking to locate in the area. The Hutterites won what they considered a landmark decision against religious discrimination.

Although Hutterites have no hesitation to retain law firms for their many financial property dealings with government and businesses, they take very seriously the biblical teaching that brother must not go to law against brother (I Cor. 6:1–8). However, even that teaching was violated recently in a bitter battle where two colonies fought one another in the provincial courts over patent rights (Jeschke 1993).

EDUCATION AND THE PUBLIC SCHOOL

The English school becomes a disruptive force when social distance is not properly maintained. In its place, the school contributes to colony cohesion. Keeping the English school "in its place" is crucial, for here is where the ideology of the world and of the colony vie for the loyalty of young minds. For the child who has not responded properly to colony indoctrination, the English school can become an important influence, leading to possible desertion. In school the child can function as an individual and learn about the world outside the colony from books and from the teacher. Intimacy between teacher and pupil can lead to defection. Friendships can lead to marriages with outsiders, to changes of denominational loyalties, and in some instances, teachers have helped young Hutterites find jobs and leave the colony. Young, single teachers, male or female, are greater risks than older teachers who are married and have children of their own.

All children of school age attend the English school on the colony. The usual pattern is for the colony to supply the building, the heating, and the maintenance costs; the school board selects and pays the salary of the teacher. The more isolated colonies may provide a small house for the teacher though fewer and fewer teachers are living in the colony. Many commute thirty or more miles a day. Whether the school is private or public, the curriculum is similar to that which is taught in rural schools. The colony makes a point of not interfering with the living pattern of the teacher, who may have a radio, a television, and a separate mailbox. The colony home of the teacher becomes an informal source of worldly knowledge to colony people and a source of intrusion if not properly controlled. Teachers who have never taught in a colony are typically given a "lecture" by the preacher at the start or with their first offense. The preacher outlines the colony's expectation of the teacher and sets the limits for practices which are "against our religion." Projected audio-visual material, television, radios, phonographs, and tape recorders are forbidden. However, some computers may occasionally be given limited acceptance. In colonies in which the school building becomes a church, the walls must be bare, the blackboard must be erased and pictures must be removed or turned to face the wall at the close of each day of school. When it is also used for the German school, the English teacher cannot work in the classroom before or after school hours. More and more colonies are utilizing a separate building, or separate classroom, used only for the English school.

The attitude toward English school is that it is important, especially in the early grades, for all children must know arithmetic and be able to use the language of the country. One leader said: "We expect our children to learn math, reading, and science as required by the Department of Education. We must learn English to understand the people around us." When asked what is most undesirable about the English school, these answers were given:

> When the teacher does not cooperate with the German teacher or the preacher; taking pictures and then distributing them to the children or when dancing is held in the school, as it happened once. Learning the worldly ways would lead to their damnation. The old physiology books were all right, but the modern health books contain too much about dating, sex education, and anatomy.

Aside from acquiring a good knowledge of arithmetic and reading, the only additional goal for Hutterites is that discipline be maintained in the English school. Teachers are expected and often encouraged to "lay down the law," and if they cannot maintain order, they are considered failures. A German teacher advised a new English teacher to "use the willow, for its the only language they understand." A complaint of teachers is that though the children are obedient, they lack self-discipline and have less respect for the outside teacher than for the German teacher. How comfortable the teacher feels often depends on how well he or she gets along with the German teacher and to what degree the English teacher understands Hutterite culture. Greater respect for the teacher can be maintained if the English school supports the prevailing authoritarian pattern.

The colony will accept the English school complex but restrain and bridle its influence so that it will serve colony ends. The school and teacherage are on the grounds, but they are oriented to one side of the colony and can function without major interference. The English school remains emotionally outside the colony. The time patterns, schedule, and colony holidays suggest superior loyalties. The first language learned and the first writing skills acquired are in German. German school is more important in a child's day than English school, as is evident from the time of day in which it meets. German school is held at the start of the day, followed by English school, and then German school meets again at the close of English school. The English school is encapsulated by the colony pattern, and ideally its influence cannot go beyond the bounds set by the culture.

One of the boundaries maintained by Hutterite culture is the use of visual equipment in the schools. In 1977 the *Lehrer-Leut* forbade the use of projectors, films, slides, tapes, radio, and television. The policy statement reads: "We recognize that the decision may not be a popular one to the many kind and well-meaning and sincere people in the Education Department who would like very much to help us. However, we could not reach another decision without violating our conscience and the trust of our Heavenly Father in the stewardship of our children."

In 1980, in response to the Department of Education in Manitoba, the *Schmied-Leut* appointed a three-member Hutterian Education Committee. Its task was to cooperate with the Multicultural Program of Canada in the development of a curriculum on Hutterite history and culture. The material was designed to make Hutterite children aware of their history and to orient teachers who come into contact with Hutterite children. The Hutterite Education Committee plans regional meetings for teachers and provides guidance in teaching the German language. Each year the committee nominates three Hutterite teachers who are sent to Germany to attend the Goethe Institute, where they receive formal instruction in teaching the German language. Most Hutterites have responded positively to the development of a social studies curriculum within the English school. A few Hutterite teachers now take college courses and acquire state certification, which enables them to teach in the colony English school.

The influence of the teacher is carefully delineated and maintained on an informal level. When the school board selects, assigns, and pays the salary of the teacher, as it does in most colony schools, the colony has little veto power if the teacher proves unsatisfactory. The teacher is given moral encouragement in ways that aid the colony pattern, mainly as a strong supporter of discipline. The teacher cannot encroach on the child's colony time pattern by asking a child to stay after school or to stay during lunch hour. A child may not be punished by depriving him of food. Discussion of a teacher's shortcomings in the presence of children limits the teacher's influence. Colonies may complain about receiving poor teachers. Indeed, some are inferior as teachers, but most of them are good teachers who enjoy teaching in colony schools. Relatively inferior academic teaching is tolerated, and teachers are virtually free from the informal supervision of superiors. There is little pressure from parents for excellence and no parental interference in teaching. However, there are limits placed by the colony on equipment and curriculum. Unlike most school teachers, who must participate and relate to the wider activities of the community, the teacher in a colony enjoys a type of privacy and freedom from such demands. The formal relations between colony adults and the teacher are cordial and are typically enhanced by gifts of food and help. Low-cost housing and eating privileges can be enjoyed by these teachers. Those teachers with cooperative attitudes, including the poorer teachers, are more readily absorbed into the environment of the colony than teachers who are aggressively competent by outside standards and demand independent thinking of their pupils. Even then, there is little danger that the teacher will become a model for the children. When the teachers emulate the colony patterns, disruption is minimized and the children tend to show greater respect for the teacher.

Attempts by Hutterites in the past to permit their own young men to enter college and acquire teacher training have largely failed. Through these attempts some of their young men in both the Ukraine and in North America deserted the colonies. Although there are presently twenty or more college-educated Hutterite men and women teaching in colony English schools, the practice is not unanimously favored. The reason as given by one spokesman is: "It is better to have the worldly school taught by a worldly person so that we can keep the lines straight."

A few Hutterite young people take correspondence courses from state colleges. Some of the teachers who are assigned to teach in the colony are willing to tutor or to give instruction beyond the elementary grades. Exploratory efforts have been made to establish high schools for Hutterite young people in regions where there are many colonies. All such efforts to take the pupils from the colony grounds have run counter to Hutterite religion and to their conceptions of child training. The Constitution of the Hutterian Brethren Church assures every child of an education in skills needed to participate in the adult community. The consequences of having to attend school beyond the time when they are accepted as adults (age fifteen) can adversely affect the individual pupil. At this age young people are given adult work privileges and serve as apprentices to skilled adults under closely supervised conditions of learning. There is a tendency for the young Hutterite to feel deprived of his or her status as a growing person when forced to attend formal schooling beyond the age required by his culture. In those few colonies that advocate continuing formal education, the young adult is not as likely to feel deprived.

The further the child goes in school, the less he is said to learn. From the colony's point of view this is correct, for once a child has mastered the basic skills, much of the rest of the subject matter learned has little relevance to their way of life. The colony German school teaches the children how to live, and the English school teaches facts, many of which are of little use to them. German school teaches proper ritual, the English school teachers worldly knowledge. The schools are clearly different, and both are regarded as necessary. In the ideal colony, there is little conflict between the two schools and the normal child receives an integrated learning experience from the viewpoint of his culture.

The disruptive influences described thus far are the major external forces affecting the colonies. These forces usually have challenged the Hutterite culture in such a way as to strengthen the dedication of its members. The internal patterns of disruption, affluence and poverty, leadership failure, defection, and deviant religious influences will now be described.

AFFLUENCE AND POVERTY

The restraints on spending money are clearly delineated in the Hutterite world view. The purpose of all wealth getting, as Rideman (1950:126) emphasized during the precapitalistic age, is that "Men should labor, working with their hands what is honest that they may have to give to him that needeth." Industriousness and thrift in Hutterite society are means to a style of life pictured by Max Weber (1930) as "ascetic Protestantism." The principle of austere consumption is consistent with the "asceticism of the sects" expressed in the refusal to use the law, to swear in courts of justice, to exercise dominion over others, or to take part in war. The "narrow path" allows no pursuit of pleasure of its own sake. The modern concept of consumer spending, in contrast with the Hutterite concept of austerity, is based on a different conception of human nature.

The dangers of wealth to Hutterites are primarily two: too much wealth and its adverse influence on a colony, and the temptations of individuals to attain either forbidden commodities or to obtain money by selling colony property. In Europe, money was accumulated and secretly concealed to carry the colonies through critical periods of war, famine, and migration. In North America, the accumulation of money outside of banks is no longer necessary, for banks have proved to be trustworthy. The major function of money is to provide capital for the expansion needed to keep pace with the population growth. Today, saving is an institutionalized pattern of all colonies, and the major incentive is to save for the time of branching. A debt-free colony with additional accumulations of money in the bank may spend it for certain extras on farm machinery, tractors, or combines. Additional machines tend to make available more positions for younger men, who are eligible for the important jobs. But too much money has certain dangers, even for the welfare of the colony. Wealthy colonies tend to obtain more labor-saving commodities, which reduces the need for manpower and womanpower on these colonies and leads to envy by others. This wealth is evidenced by a high degree of mechanization, especially for the work of women, which is usually the last phase of mechanization. Serger sewing machines and microwave ovens are presently the exception rather than the rule. A certain amount of consumer goods can be permitted if all share equally, but the danger is in its effect on other colonies and the individuals themselves, whose wants are increased.

A wealthy colony that fails to branch can prove disruptive to the communal way of life. Excessive wealth with unresolved conflicts between informal factions has led to disruption. The reason for not branching is that "the colony becomes too content" with its financially prosperous reputation and with its "luxuries," and there is added complication of not being able to agree to branch or to resolve the problem of polarization that may exist between brother sibships.

Colony wealth tends to have an influence on the marriage patterns. With colony affluence, there emerges what Hutterites call "girl power"—the tendency for girls to put off marriage for a number of years to enjoy the conveniences of their own colony. Few girls are fortunate enough to obtain a husband in their own colony since patrilocal rule requires that girls join the colony of their husbands. In a prosperous colony, prestige reaches a point that is rather atypical for the colonies as a whole. The ascetic restraints on consumption are slightly modified to allow for the enjoyment of small luxuries. The girls say, "Why should we get married, we have it so good here." Thus, marriage is put off until the late twenties, just short of the "old maid" stage. Were this practice to become widespread, there would likely be a marked decline in the number of children born to a family. A colony of poor reputation, whether through chronic drought or poverty or mismanagement, also has marriage problems. A boy receives no encouragement from his parents to marry a girl who belongs to a colony with a poor standing, and no girl wants to marry into a poor colony.

Individuals who receive private income beyond the small allowances given by the colony are a potential threat to the ideals and practices of the colony. Unauthorized money can be gained privately in several ways, and it is a perpetual problem for the colony leadership. Laboring for a nearby farmer during evening hours is one source of income. Money can be obtained by selling or trading colony property: a duck, turkey, chicken, or a bottle of colony wine, with outsiders. If caught the offender will be punished. Women sometimes sew for outsiders, and women in several colonies have held "garage sales."

Trapping is a tempting and occasionally a profitable private enterprise. Young boys of school age will trap animals like rabbits that can be caught with little effort, while older boys catch cunning animals and those with the more valuable furs. Groups of school-age boys will assist each other in the activity and will exclude those not of their age or clique. Frozen rabbits can be accumulated in the very cold winter until an older, unbaptized person will take them to town for a cash price. A boy has been known to catch twenty-five rabbits in a single winter. One boy, in one season, trapped 150 muskrats worth $1 each, and he also caught several beavers and mink. Suspicious mail that comes to the colony is opened by the preacher or the parents. To overcome this barrier, boys who are assigned to prolonged jobs away from the colony's buildings, like herding sheep or bulldozing, will rent a personal post-office box. For a nominal fee, a box can be secured in a town not usually patronized by the colony. Furs may be shipped to faraway places, and through mail order, the boys can secure transistor radios and other private but forbidden property. The small, secretive adolescent clique can often do an effective business until the subversion is discovered. All of this in the Hutterite view attests to man's natural, selfish desire and with baptism all such subversiveness must be confessed. The consequences of not confessing all previous sins can be disastrous. One young man who had in his youth left the colony and returned was ordained as preacher. He was liked by most colonists and achieved a very favorable status. After several years, his secret sins began to bother him. He confessed that he had earned money while outside, invested it, and was still collecting interest. He was excommunicated for one week and permanently relieved of his position.

In some of the fringe colonies there is a tendency for young men to accumulate savings with which to buy furnishings for the home after marriage. In still other colonies, savings secured by working for neighbors are accumulated by family heads. This practice leads to serious consequences for the colony as a whole since it introduces differentiation between families. The family-allowance benefits available to family heads in Canada have been disruptive. For example, monthly allowance for each child under age eighteen can provide a substantial income for a Hutterite family. When some families receive the government benefits and others do not, there is ill-feeling among families. Some colonies permit families to receive the benefits, but the funds go into the colony account. Preachers' conferences, however, have ruled that the practice is too disruptive for the welfare of the colonies.

To the Hutterite, private wealth is a means by which the individual can be drawn away from his proper spiritual relationship. Luxury must be avoided. The temporal life of the individual must be controlled by the spiritual order. Thus, while material goods are necessary for the body, they must not become the object of pleasure. The human body itself is important only because it houses the soul that is capable of establishing an eternal relationship with God.

LEADERSHIP FAILURE

The prime leadership role in a colony is that of the first preacher. He heads the council, which is responsible for the implementation of policy made by his own colony and by the preacher assembly which ordained him. In decision making his vote counts no more than others, but his recommendations carry added weight. In its routine affairs a colony is autonomous; decisions, once brought to vote, are decided by majority. If there is mismanagement within a colony, any member may "complain to the elders," the preacher assembly. The preachers will conduct an investigation and intervene where a leader is believed to be guilty of misconduct. A preacher can be deposed from office. A preacher who neglects to elect a householder in a colony can be ordered to do so by the preacher assembly. Ideally, every member is led by the Holy Spirit and will vote persons into office whom he believes are best qualified.

Disruption of a colony is possible through "poor" leaders and through "bad" leaders. Poor leaders lack native ability and training sufficient to the task; bad leaders lack integrity and use colony resources or their position for personal or family gain. Rivalry for leadership between the preacher and the householder is possible, but long experience has defined very clearly the role and relationship of each. The Chronicle warns householders, especially, against the temptations of selfishness, the desire to dominate, and the tendency toward laziness. Not only is the householder to be subject to the church and the preacher, but all of the varied stewards are to guard their work and resources carefully. In modern times it is unlikely, but possible, for a householder to squander the money of the colony through excessive drinking, even gambling, and unwise investments made without the consent of the colony. Any such offenses are reviewed and punished by the preacher assembly. On the informal level, a householder is often the son or brother of the preacher, and any tendencies toward rivalry or extortion are minimal.

There is little a colony can do to remove a "weak" leader if he does not commit a flagrant transgression. When a "bad" leader arises, there is usually a factionalization of the colony into dominant family lines that vie for power. Often, the early elements of this factionalization have culminated in the selection of a "bad" leader. If a colony is already factionalized into competing families, there is little a strong, capable leader can do to correct the situation, other than to attempt to lead with a strong hand and to plan for an early branching. If an incapable leader is selected, the total structure of a healthy colony may carry it through this period of weak leadership. Similarly, most cohesive colonies can survive the tenure of a poor householder if the other members of the council are capable leaders. In some cases, the preacher assembly will step in to mitigate the situation. This is supportive and remedial.

Informal power struggles between groups of families can lead to disruption. When formal power is wrested from the colony by the nuclear family, or a group of families, usually a group of grown brothers, there can be serious cleavages. Colonies will rank each other by such factors as wealth, degrees of mechanization, managerial ability, amount and kind of defection by individuals, reputation of the preacher, and the degree of conformity to rules. Variations in these characteristics are to be expected. Some colonies that appear to be cohesive and well-managed to the outsider may actually be suffering from chronic internal troubles. Rarely do colonies resort to courts of law to settle internal conflicts. Yet, in the case of cleavages along family lines, several suits over property ownership have been brought to the courts. Usually they occur among factions who have refused the advice of the judicial preacher assembly. In one unusual case, four brothers and their families, of a total of seven families in a colony, accepted a Protestant faith. The brothers refused to leave the colony and asked the court to dissolve the colony corporation and distribute the assets among the seven families. The court ruled against the brothers. The 1993 constitution addresses some of the problems of leadership failure.

Ideally, each nuclear family is subordinate to the welfare of the colony. In practice, a colony may be polarized between two or more sets of older brothers who hold important offices. Their mothers, more than their wives, are important in the informal leadership pattern. To maintain balance on the informal level, the role of women is crucial, for they must be socialized to "accept their place." Since women are believed to be inferior to men physically, intellectually, and emotionally, they must obey and follow their husbands. Through marriage, women unite (or form a link between) different family lines. This introduces an extended set of loyalties into the husband's family, which checks the exclusiveness of blood-brother relationships. The woman is more oriented toward her family of procreation than to her family of orientation, although she maintains a loyalty to and a relationship with her parents and her sisters and brothers. She supports her husband in his competition with her brothers and with his brothers, and she always supports her grown sons. The man tends to maintain a deeper loyalty to his family of orientation than to his family of procreation. The differing loyalties of the husband and wife function to prevent the nuclear family from becoming too strong. Any aggression the wife may feel against her husband for his seeming lack of emotional support is channeled against men in general and helps maintain a division between the male subculture and female subculture that functions to minimize sexual intrigue in a society that lives in close physical proximity. The woman's loyalty to the woman's subculture also offsets the emotional importance of the nuclear family, in much the same way as the man's identification with the colony as a whole supersedes and thus weakens his personal identification with his wife and children.

Women have no voting privileges and no institutionalized means for acquiring formal leadership positions. Therefore, when women become powerful in intra-colony politics, it is usually through an emphasis on the consanguineal family, rather than on the good of the colony as a whole. When a preacher or householder is said to be strict, it generally means that he is strict in keeping women in their place. Within the present Hutterite culture this contributes to the smooth functioning of the colony as a unit, for it protects the society from self-centered, competing family groups.

DEFECTION

Several types of defection from the colony are disruptive to the social structure. There are individuals (usually young, unbaptized men) who "try the world" for several weeks or months, perhaps by following the harvest, but who return to colony life. There are a relatively small number of these "tourists" to the outside world who desert the colony permanently. Another type of defection is characterized by a group of "discontents" who defect from the traditional faith and give allegiance to some competing "renewal" group.

Since their migration to North America, relatively few persons have reacted against the Hutterite system by abandoning it completely. The tendency for defections to increase in recent years does, however, give the elders concern. Only 258 men and 11 women left the colony voluntarily from 1880 to 1951, according to Eaton and Weil (1955:146), but over half returned; 106 men and 8 women were permanent defectors. Among the *Schmied-Leut* to 1960, 98 men and 7 women had defected (Mange 1963:32). An extensive study of factors associated with defection made by the authors leads them to conclude that the socialization patterns are so effective that the small number who do abandon the colonies are those who were disadvantaged or deprived of the normal training given a child.

The number of people who abandon colony life is highly correlated with a "declining" (as opposed to a cohesive) colony and can be accounted for in a few sibships. A declining colony (or as the Hutterites call it, *ein sterbene Kolonie)* has chronic problems of internal leadership that have not been resolved. The oldest colonies appear to have more structural problems than the newly established colonies. The mobility pattern does not permit a member to move from his home colony to another colony. Thus, persons may not abandon a declining colony to join a more desirable one. Many of those who defected permanently had experienced long-term disputes with the householder, the preacher, or the German teacher. Leaving the colony, in most cases, was premeditated and touched off by arguments or antagonisms with superiors.

The Hutterites believe that defection occurs largely in certain "weak" or "liberal" family lines. This view of defection among themselves is valid, for of 38 defectors interviewed it was found that half originated in five families and all were located in declining colonies. The high status accorded to some families (usually those in leadership positions) and low status accorded to others were marked in these colonies. Nepotism was common in a declining colony, and discrimination was invariably felt by the low-status individuals and families. The parents of many of those who abandoned the colony were atypical in some way: the relationship of the sons to their father was abnormal—either the father was very authoritarian or he showed favoritism toward one son. Out of a group of 38 defectors, 11 were the sons of either preachers or householders. In a family where the father had been deposed as householder, 7 children had defected from the colony.

Hidden competition for roles is normal, but it can become abnormal when one family represented on the council has too great an influence. There is some tendency toward primogeniture and inheritance of roles because a son, usually the oldest, acquires an intimate knowledge of the work of his father. The tendency toward role inheritance is functional. The cattle man for example, must have the knowledge and ability to compete with the market conditions outside of the colony. It is important that the son know everything his father knew about cattle, and he must improve upon this knowledge. Strained relations between father and son can thus diminish the economic efficiency of the colony. Discontent is enhanced if the traditional roles are not equitably distributed among sibships.

When an adult or a leader flirts with alien values, the effect on the younger ones will be pronounced. The young, unbaptized man in a declining colony gets little help from his peers if he has ambitions of restoring order and the earlier idealism of his colony. Since adolescents are believed to be naturally "young and unproven," there is a particular problem in such a colony to maintain the traditional respect for authority. The discrepancy that develops between belief and practice will, for example, allow a person to have a radio, but he must not be caught listening to it.

Daughters have very different role strains than do sons. They share the subordinate status placed on women. If a family has a good reputation, the daughter has a good chance of an early marriage and does not feel the need to be pre-eminent or to rebel. Even though few women leave the colony, there is evidence that daughters of leaders do face atypical problems. All colony roles are psychologically marked by strong elements of dependency, but especially so for women. Any woman who cannot accept the definition of the role given to her will have more difficulty than a man in finding alternative avenues of expression. Several groups of sisters who abandoned a colony gave as their reasons that the colony was no longer Christian. An underlying factor is that these sisters, who found company in each other's misery, rejected the submissive Hutterite role assigned to women. Their conversion to an individualistically oriented fundamentalist denomination permitted a rational way of escape.

Overemphasis on the individual constitutes a disruptive influence in a communal society. It is rare that an individual will receive sufficient personal attention so that he will develop adequate personal security to leave the protective environment of the colony. Parents who show favoritism to a child or entertain ambitions for a child beyond those sanctioned by the colony introduce dissident elements and increase the probability of defection. This relationship is vaguely understood by Hutterites, who say that if one is too good to a single child he is more likely to leave. The favored child, who obtains attention and privilege above others in the family or in the colony, acquires self-confidence above his peers. Interests are developed and needs are felt beyond what the colony can provide. A child that does not experience the same rejection as his peers will not be frightened by problems that require imagination and individual solution. A father who wanted his son to become an engineer (a goal not attained by others in the colony) entertained noncolony goals for him. A father who wanted his son to become the English school teacher on the colony entertained a vocation for him that led to defection. When such an expectation is supported by the colony, it is less disruptive, for the welfare of the colony remains the primary goal. An able leader who exceeds the limits (usually intellectually) or engages in certain privileges may unwaringly pave the way for subsequent deviation by his children. When children are treated as separate personalities in the formative years, individualism tends to develop to such an extent that it constitutes a threat to the colony. The system works best when the pre-eminence of the collective welfare over individual welfare is cheerfully and unquestionably accepted by all the members.

With few exceptions, the defectors interviewed were single when they left the colony and found homes for themselves in predominantly rural areas. They found work similar to that performed in the colony. Very few moved directly into urban centers. Most of the defectors have become farm laborers rather than owners. Several are welders, a skill they acquired on the colony. Most are highly motivated in their job performance. The male defectors tended to be inactive or indifferent to religion. They showed little interest in making distinctions among the vast number of denominations that are not Hutterite. The absolutist position of the Hutterite religion continues to structure the thinking patterns of those who defect permanently. The religion taught to them in childhood is basically respected by them in such statements as: "If I ever want religion, I know where to find it." One who had abandoned the colony forty years ago said that during the intervening years, "The little faith that you had was right there to sort of guide you. The guardian angel was always with you, it seemed like."

THE SOCIETY OF BROTHERS

Eberhard Arnold (1883-1935), founder of the Society of Brothers, was a German theologian who, as a result of his studies and personal commitment, founded a small movement in 1920 that was devoted to communal living and was influenced by sixteenth century Hutterite writings. On learning that there were Hutterites in North America, he spent an entire year, 1930, visiting all the existing 30 colonies.

The Hutterites were favorably impressed with Arnold's devotion and sincerity. His knowledge of Hutterite history, his facility with the German language, his interest in communal living, and his manner of dress, including the wearing of a beard, undoubtedly helped Arnold in his search for unification. In December of 1930 Arnold was ordained by the Hutterite elders, "To proclaim the word of God and establish the faith in Germany." Arnold returned to Germany with the financial and spiritual support of the Hutterite church. He also took with him to Germany many of their oldest manuscripts preserved for centuries in the colonies. His intention was to publish and reprint basic Hutterite source material.

Arnold died unexpectedly in 1935. His community was suppressed by German National Socialism. Two Hutterite elders from the United States visited the German *Bruderhof* in 1937, just in time to see their property confiscated by the Nazis (Durnbaugh 1991:67). The survivors of the *Bruderhof* moved from Germany to Liechtenstein and then to England. Under heavy pressure from the British government, who feared that resident German nationals might aid in a possible invasion, the Society of Brothers migrated to Paraguay in 1940-1942. Attempts to migrate to the United States or Canada and locate near the Hutterite colonies failed. Hutterites supported the communities in Paraguay in hopes that they would become faithful members of the traditional Hutterite church. The distance between Paraguay and the Hutterite colonies in North America was too great for close integration and cooperation.

When the Hutterites learned that the Paraguayan communities were violating Hutterite standards of conduct, two elders were sent to Paraguay to have a "heart to heart talk." The two groups of elders met in conference and found differences that could not be negotiated. Distressing to the North American elders were these practices: the custom of smoking, the uncovered heads of the young girls, not folding hands for prayer, singing instead of praying before and after meals, and sermons which lacked biblical substance. After the delegates from America returned home and reported their findings to the assembly of preachers (1955), the Hutterite leaders terminated their support of the Paraguayan communities and excluded them as members of the Hutterian Church. The Society of Brothers established their first colony in the United States in 1954. Serious internal conflicts during the 1960's lead to the termination of their Paraguayan communities. The economic basis of the Society of Brothers is not agricultural but the manufacture of toys and equipment for handicapped persons. The headquarters of their several locations is Woodcrest Community, Rifton, New York.

For two decades following 1974 the *Arnold-Leut*, as the Hutterites called the Society of Brothers, and the traditional Hutterites renewed their fellowship. At this time the Society of Brothers took the name Hutterite or Hutterian Brethren. By 1991 this relationship was once again being called into question. Issues related to authoritarianism among the *Schmied-Leut* in both religious matters and investments. For a time the *Schmied-Leut* and the *Arnold-Leut* remained in close contact, while both were being censored by the *Lehrer-Leut* and the *Darius-Leut*. By the mid-nineties problems relating to investments, patent rights and a mission colony in Africa were undermining the cooperative relationship between the *Schmied-Leut* and the *Arnold-Leut*. The continued use of the name Hutterite or Hutterian Brethren has been opposed by the traditional Hutterites and has created confusion about the identity of the two groups. In speaking for his traditional, four-century-old Hutterian church, one Hutterite leader expressed the view of many: "Our two cultures should not be blended because each is distinctive and incompatible. It is our wish that the Society's members serve God in their own unique way and leave us to serve Him as we see best." (Kleinsasser 1994).

For further reading on the differences in world view between the two groups, the reader may consult the bibliography. See especially Arnold (1964), Zablocki (1980) and Samuel Kleinsasser (1994). For views of those who have left the Society of Brothers see KIT (Keep In Touch), a monthly newsletter published by the Peregrine Foundation, San Francisco.

6 / The Genius of the Culture

This case study has focused on those aspects of the culture central to Hutterite society. The background of the culture and its location in time was discussed in the Introduction. A chapter each was devoted to world view, colony lifestyle, technology and economic practices, socialization and family, and disruptive patterns. In this concluding chapter, the genius of the culture will be assessed. By genius is meant the native ability of the society to survive, to adapt to its environment, to meet the problems created by its own culture, and to provide for the basic human needs of the individuals in the community.

Discussed here is traditional Hutterite culture and not those communities that have deliberately opted for change in basic beliefs and behavior patterns. In general, the *Schmied-Leut* colonies have shown greater indications of change than either the *Lehrer-Leut* or the *Darius-Leut*. The culture demonstrates a unique social adaptation to a high rate of natural increase. The population characteristics of Hutterite society resemble that of a stable population model (Eaton and Mayer, 1954). The age-sex distribution within the group has remained fairly constant during its entire period in North America. Until the 1960s, the birth rate and death rates remained relatively constant. The population continues to be overwhelmingly youthful, but not in the usual "primitive way" characterized by a high birth rate and a high infant death rate. The proportion of young children in the total population remains high due to a consistently high birth rate. Adults have about the normal life expectancy, but old people are a small minority because of the successive waves of new children. Thus, the fertility rate resembles that of underdeveloped countries, but the mortality pattern resembles that of industrialized countries. The high rate of natural increase requires appropriate social organization, flexibility, and expansion to meet these conditions.

The Hutterite society approximates the conditions required of any society to maintain a continuous high rate of population growth. These conditions include: (1) a stable society which is highly structured, (2) resources and factors favorable to expansion, and (3) a value system prescribing a high fertility rate (Lorimer et al 1954). The high fertility rate creates social problems which can be solved only through access to sufficient resources: in this case, the acquisition of land and the accumulation of capital. Capital is accumulated by work and modes of behavior that are severely patterned. The values support a high fertility pattern and at the same time engender motivations that include sufficient spiritual and material rewards. Despite Hutterite ideology, there is evidence that family size has begun to decline. One study of Hutterite fertility control (Ingoldsby and Stanton 1988) concludes that a great many Hutterites are now using artificial means of birth control.

A Hutterite boy and girl.

Typically, most sects and subcultures are forced to change their social structure as the population expands. With the coming of industrialization and Western influence, many aboriginal bands of people in North America fled or disintegrated because they were unwilling to adapt their economy to the requirements of agriculture and a sedentary life. The Hutterites have not only fully accepted mechanized agriculture, but have adapted to a high rate of population increase by their institution of branching, which allows new units of the society to develop. The most significant social unit, the colony, is firmly controlled in size and location in a manner that prevents urbanism and merchandising. Each colony is a primary social unit consisting of several nuclear families in a face-to-face group.

Hutterite society exhibits a remarkably stable pattern of communal living. Of all communal groups in the United States, the Hutterites are the largest, have the longest history, and are the most successful in maintaining communal life. There have been many attempts at communal living in the United States. Most of these have been short-lived. Of 130 communal-type settlements, 91 lasted less than a decade, 59 less than five years, 50 only two years, and 32 only one year (Deets 1939:22). Four endured for a century or more and are now virtually extinct. They were the Amana Society, the Ephrata Cloister, the Shakers, and Old Economy. The Doukhobors, who organized in Russia in the eighteenth century, settled in western Canada in 1879, and are still living in several cooperative communities. When the Hutterites came to the

United States in 1874, there were eight different communal societies in 72 separate colonies. During the ensuing years, all eight societies have declined or completely vanished as social systems, while the Hutterites have grown from three to over 382 colonies.

The explanation of the stable social pattern is multifaceted. The goal of the society to live communally is achieved through a combination of factors. The most pervasive of these are acceptance of supernatural authority, a dualistic view of nature sanctioning separation from the world with a tendency toward isolation, limited addition of new members other than offspring, and a willingness to die or be killed rather than change their basic beliefs and social institutions. Supernatural authority is incarnated in the colony authority pattern. The belief that divine order governs material and social relationships is learned in infancy, perpetuated throughout life, and acknowledged on the deathbed. The ordered universe is conceived as hierarchical, with one part always submissive to the other. The lower obeys and serves the higher. The higher directs and cares for the lower. Central beliefs are unusually explicit about goals, subgoals, and norms of practice, and have a high degree of internal consistency. There is no speculation about theology, and logical thought and reasoned solutions are applied mainly to the economic activities of making a living. The basic ideology is supported by appropriate ritual, constant teaching, highly patterned social relationships, and clear delineation between power that may be democratically managed by man and power that is exercised only by God. The central beliefs appear to be sufficiently comprehensive to satisfy individual inquisitiveness within the scope of the colony environment.

The dualistic view of human nature, spiritual and carnal, is pervasive in the social organization and becomes the reasoned basis for separation from the world. The activities of the colony, the training of the young, and the management of specific problems are approached by the predetermined spiritual, rather than carnal, assumptions. The deification of social unity on a subverbal level and the submission of the self to the will of God tends to minimize arguments and speculations of a theological nature. Geographic isolation as well as symbolic isolation through language and dress are manifestations of the central belief in separation from the world. Isolation effectively minimizes the problems of communal living as the Hutterites practice it.

The small number of nonethnic converts to the colonies is conducive to a stable social pattern. The practice of sending out missionaries to preach and make converts outside of the community in their early period of history has been discontinued. This practice eliminates the problems of assimilating large numbers of outsiders. As the Hutterite movement became institutionalized and strongly patterned, the group relied on its own offspring for new members. In its charismatic or prophetic stage the movement attracted converts, but during the seventeenth century the group tended toward institutionalization.

Hutterite child rearing and socialization practices are phenomenally successful in preparing the individual for communal life. The individual is taught to be obedient, submissive, and dependent upon human support and contact. Socialization is consistent and continuous in all age groups. From early childhood to adulthood there is no relaxation of indoctrination within clearly defined age and sex groupings. Every individual is subservient to the colony at every stage of life. The goals for each

Nurturant behavior, sharing and affection are encouraged. Hutterite children are seldom alone and never deprived of food.

stage are attainable. Individuals are well-trained to meet clearly defined roles, and each is rewarded by the smooth execution of his or her work and by the awareness that his or her contribution is needed by the colony. A certain amount of deviance of an acceptable type is permitted within each age set and relieves the system of stifling rigidity.

Hutterite children learn a great deal about the authority structure of their society and how to live comfortably within it. They internalize the Hutterite hierarchy, but they also learn that the authority of each individual is limited. Children are never punished by depriving them of food or nurturance. Work is never used as punishment, for there is no colony work that is categorized as unpleasant, and everyone must be willing to do cheerfully any type of work that is assigned. Privileges are not withheld from a naughty child. If the group goes on an excursion to help butcher sheep or brand cattle, the erring child goes too. If it is that child's turn to visit another colony, when the truck is going he or she may go no matter how recent or serious the misbehavior.

Socialization is achieved in a supernaturally based authority system. All elements of knowledge, motivation, and activity are directly related to a single source of authority and are subordinated to it. No segment of knowledge remains unrelated to the dominant source of authority, nor is any permitted to develop aside from it. The scope of socialization includes a conception of time that is temporal as well as eternal and involves the active participation of the individual in both. Ritualization of temporal and sacred activity is well-proportioned. The individual is socialized within a spatial relationship that includes all of the social institutions, activities, and resources needed for the individual. Interaction with and dependency upon outsiders is minimized.

In infancy the children learn to enjoy people and to respond positively to many persons. After age three they are weaned away from their nuclear family and learn to accept authority in virtually any form. They learn that aloneness is associated with unpleasant experiences and that being with others is rewarded with pleasant experiences. During the school years they are further weaned from their family. They learn more about authority, and acquire a verbal knowledge of their religion. They acquire the ability to relate positively to their peer group and to respond to its demands. As small children their universe is unpredictable, but as they mature in their peer group and take part in colony life their universe becomes highly predictable. They learn to minimize self-assertion and self-confidence and to establish dependence on the group. As members of a categorically defined age set, the young children learn explicitly when and whom to obey. School-age children receive limited companionship and little indulgence from their parents; they learn how their peer group protects and punishes them; they learn to accept frustrations passively, and to enjoy hard physical labor. When children become adults, they are rewarded with responsibility, privileges, and greater recognition and acceptance by their own nuclear family. After becoming a full member of the colony through baptism, the self-image expands to include identification with the whole colony.

The expectations for the individual within the social structure are clearly defined by the ideology and are reinforced by the social patterns. Each individual knows what is expected of him or her; each wants to follow these expectations and, in most instances, is able to do so. The individual Hutterite identifies ideologically and emotionally with the colony system. There is a strong aversion to the ways of the *Draussiger,* the outsider, who is a child of the world. Hutterites look at themselves as belonging, not to a world created by Newton, Beethoven, Sartre, or Einstein, but to the model described in the Bible. The colony is, as for certain other ascetic Christian groups, a paradise surrounded by vast numbers of unconverted human beings whose destiny is determined by God and whom the individual Hutterite will not judge.

The ascetic demand of the society does not ask the individual to mortify the basic human drives, but to subject them to a community of love that is both human and divine. Sex is managed in such a way that it is not a threat to the reproductive patterns, as with some communal Christian groups. In its socially sanctioned place, the practice of sex is distinguished from the "lust of the eye," which is illegitimate desire. Sex is limited to married pairs, and there is no evidence of any tendency toward celibacy or continence after marriage. Families are generally happy and supportive of the colony's superior power position. As an individual, a Hutterite may demonstrate what appears to the outside as egocentrism or pride. But to the Hutterite, who knows that their system is right, he or she is not expressing personal pride but simply a state of mind that has no doubts. The emotional identification with the colony is evidenced by the number who return after "trying the world" and the relatively few who permanently desert the colony.

An ordained preacher and four of his children.

The Hutterite appraisal of human nature is functional in the communal system. In some respects, it is dynamic. A child's nature is regarded as carnal (selfish) and mush be supplanted by the spiritual (selfless) nature. The spiritual nature is expressed within a social hierarchy that is based on moral obligations among the members. The Hutterites regard the child's personality as intrinsically good only as the child (behaviorally) gives up his or her individual will and conforms voluntarily to the will of the colony. The consequences of this appraisal of human nature for delinquent individuals is somewhat opposed to that of contemporary society in North America. When a Hutterite youth transgresses the rules, the youth will be punished, but not because he or she was bad. Since the society knows everyone is bad from the start, it is required that the wrongdoer suffer the consequences of misbehavior. The society expects that the badness will, with maturity, be supplanted by responsibility. The adolescent who occasionally transgresses the rules can still see himself as being on the road toward goodness. Hutterite society makes it a point to forgive when true signs of betterment are observed. These manifestations are encouraged and rewarded. When individuals become full members, they are obligated to teach and uphold the morality of Hutterite society.

In North American society, by contrast, the child is thought of as good, primarily needing a chance for self-development and self-realization. When the child transgresses the rules of the society, the child is disappointing. The adolescent who comes into conflict with the law tends to be labeled as bad and this label will stain his or her future reputation. Transgression has a certain irreversible and unredemptive direction, and the road to goodness becomes almost exclusively the task of the individual. The Hutterite practice tends toward the acceptance of deviancy within manageable proportions, frequently within a small peer group. The Hutterite position is simply that the individual is not perfect and cannot attain perfection without the aid of all the colony members. The net effect is a view of the individual that leads toward rehabilitation with a minimum of condemnation. The Hutterite individual knows why he or she is alive, knows how he or she should live, and subjectively feels able to meet the standards of behavior.

Innovation without acculturation: innovation is selective, managed, and tends to be consistent from the viewpoint of the dominant goal of communal living. Innovation does not alter the internal hierarchy and social structure. As in all societies, culture change among Hutterites is selective and proceeds according to a pattern that is more or less consistent with their world view. Innovations are evaluated with reference to the basic objectives of communal living. Changes in material culture are more acceptable than changes in value patterns or beliefs. Colonies today engage in more large-scale specialized agriculture and small-scale manufacturing than they did thirty years ago. The presence of large equipment, trucks, tractors, combines, and swathers indicates greater mechanization. Large harvesters that can produce up to 12,000 bushels of grain in an hour are discussed enthusiastically. Field equipment and trucks may have two-way radios or cellular telephones. Several photocopy machines may be found in a single colony. Objection to picture taking has become rare. The use of battery-operated golf carts by supervisors and older people in the colony is accepted.

Changes in hairstyles and grooming are especially noticeable among unbaptized boys and girls. In some colonies boys will wear belts instead of suspenders, Western hats and boots, or will go without hats. Some of the girls have modified their hairstyle slightly and the way in which they tie their polka-dotted covering. The use of cosmetics among girls is more evident than it was two decades ago. The rate of defection by both boys and girls is a continuing concern. The Hutterites ability to adapt to change is important to their survival in the modern world. The past migrations of the group, with their strong preference for living in countries and in regions geographically isolated from large urban centers, have minimized many of the complex problems brought about by change. When the external pressures became too great in the past, the group has moved to other lands.

Innovations in the colonies are carefully considered and evaluated on the basis of their possible effect on communal living. Informal talk always precedes any formal discussion of change. Modernity is not necessarily stereotyped as being evil or worldly. Most leaders fail to acknowledge any conflict between religious beliefs and technological change. "Nothing is too modern if it is profitable for the colony." The dominant criterion for introducing change is whether the innovation supports the welfare of the colony. A firm boundary is drawn between changes that involve the economic well-being of the whole colony and changes that are primarily for personal comfort and convenience. "We do not believe in making everything nice for the flesh," they say. Installing showers (in addition to tubs that they already had) in the central laundry required more time and discussion in one colony than buying a new combine. Changes are considered safe when they are anchored on spiritual rather than carnal grounds. Innovations in the outside world, by contrast, are believed to be made on the basis of satisfying the carnal nature of man. Changes are spaced, as too many changes at one time are not considered good for the colony. Even more important for survival than "controlled acculturation" (Eaton 1952) is the necessity that all members share alike in any changes permitted. In this way the relative status of any one individual to others has not changed at all. No person is made richer or poorer or more powerful than others. The preacher is still the spiritual leader, the younger are still subordinate to the older, and women are still subject to rule by men. The use of trucks, tractors, mechanized poultry and computerized hog production in the colony, and the introduction of sewing machines and electric irons have not changed the social relationships. The Hutterites adjust to a changing technology, but they would rather die than change their basic social patterns, which they believe to be ordered by supernatural authority.

Hutterites maximize the power of informal, primary group consensus. The daily, constant association between leaders and followers, among persons of all ages, tends toward solidarity and an intimate knowledge of the values and opinions held by other persons. Normative practices tend to develop and determine the issues that will be

A colony-made lake provides recreation and illustrates modernizing trends in social behavior as well as economic activities.

discussed formally. Nothing is discussed formally that is not already a problem or an issue of concern to the group. When there is pressure for change on the part of the foreman and managers, the leaders are able to assess it informally, and after there is widespread informal agreement, the colony formally votes on an issue. Decisions are made on the basis of a majority vote. The acceptance of innovations by consensus before there is widespread breaking of the rules and before pressures become unmanageable has the effect of maintaining members' respect for the authority system. The emphasis on group welfare and de-emphasis on individual rights and convictions minimizes the friction often associated with innovation in sectarian societies.

On the formal level, individual colonies may allow only those changes that are in keeping with the preacher assembly. A given colony is not autonomous but is subject to the discipline (*Gemeindeordnungen*) of the preacher assembly. These rules perpetuate uniformity among colonies, and slow down the rate of innovation. The balance in decision making between any given colony and its preacher assembly appears to have great advantages in terms of satisfying human needs. When one or more colonies deviate from a formal disciplinary rule, the preacher assembly will place the issue on their agenda. The violation may be discussed and the rule that was violated may be reaffirmed by majority vote; it may be modified, or a vote may be postponed to allow time for further informal consensus. Issues of special concern to the preacher assembly result in a formal statement, which is circulated and read to all colonies by their preacher. The colonies, in turn, vote whether to accept the ruling. Thus, while the Hutterites give their complete loyalty to a theocratic rule, the rules that govern behavior are democratically managed. The reason for changes are neither individual wants nor expediency, but are based entirely on the welfare of the colony.

Cleavages that normally develop between competing families or individuals for acquiring property in North American society have no formal basis for existence in Hutterite society. Material innovations are managed so as not to be disruptive. Family units are not competing against each other for wealth. When a colony is prosperous, the family units benefit equally, and none are symbolically excluded. Wealth, property, and knowledge are denied as a means of social distinction. The competition that is often very marked between colonies is integrative rather than disruptive to any given colony. Any impression, however, that the colonies express no anxiety about the effects of change would be misleading. The contacts engendered by commerce and trade with the large urban centers near their colonies can have undesirable consequences for them.

Through its many self-sustaining colony units, Hutterite society is sufficiently patterned to integrate the meaning of economic values with spiritual values. Each colony is a believing community, a community of worship, and a community of work. The absolutism of their ideology has made it necessary for them to migrate to various countries, where they have tended to live in isolation from their neighbors. The ideology has not forced the members to isolate themselves from biologic, economic, and technological solutions to living. The group has retained vital links between the generations. In shaping patterns within the culture, the group has managed the problems of fragmentation, of individualistic and dictatorial leaders, defection, and senile decay. The bond of community is defined in such a way as to include the physical and emotional components of human need. The deep feeling for the correctness of their way of life was expressed by a thoughtful Hutterite who said: "If there will ever be a perfect culture it may not be exactly like the Hutterites—but it will be similar."

Appendix A / Fieldwork in a Communal Society

EDITORIAL INTRODUCTION

The difference between participant and nonparticipant observation becomes strikingly clear in this Appendix as John Hostetler and Gertrude Huntington describe their roles in interaction with Hutterites and in the communal colonies where their field research was carried out. The full cooperation and support of the people in the colonies was secured because the authors respected Hutterite norms for demeanor and behavior. John Hostetler, with his Amish background, was accepted as akin to the Hutterites in general cultural and personality orientation. Gertrude Huntington and her family conformed, in nearly every detail, to Hutterite norms, and lived and worked within the role definitions appropriate to a family of no particular distinction within the colony.

From her description of her and her family's roles, the compressive quality of life in a tightly organized communal society as seen by an outsider becomes vividly clear. The rewards are sufficiently high so that the community keeps its membership, and it is efficient as a productive unit so that its economic base is sound. The "cost accounting" of the cultural system is in sharp limitation of individual freedom, independence, and individualism in general. The gains are security, both economic and personal. The Hutterite colonies, like Zuni Pueblos, are at one extreme of communalism. North American society, in terms of its dominant ethos, is at another extreme of individualism.

This chapter helps us to understand not only how anthropological fieldwork can take place in a tightly organized communal society but also the nature of that society.

Both of the authors were asked to reply to the question, "How did you happen to come into anthropology?"

> I turned from an early career in poultry judging and poultry husbandry to a career in understanding man because I decided that people were more interesting and more in need of understanding than turkeys. I knew nothing of anthropology until I entered graduate training. Once having been exposed to some of its principles and the fervent honesty of my teachers, I took all the courses my schools offered. This, combined with fieldwork in American communities, including my mother-culture (Old Order Amish), has helped me to understand from culture "how moderns got that way."
>
> —John A. Hostetler

My inclination toward anthropology probably began in my childhood. When I was ten years old, I visited the Cuna Indians off the coast of Panama with a shipload of tourists. I

Author John Hostetler examines rare manuscripts with a Hutterite couple.

was the first white female child most of the women had seen. They fingered my hair and clothes, pulling the decorations and buttons off my dress, and gave me presents of necklaces and hen's eggs. When French and English children lived in our home during the Second World War, we argued the merits of differing conventions—American, English, French, and even African.

After a year of graduate training in genetics and some research on twinning, I worked in a predominantly Morman region of Wyoming and then taught school in Turkey for two years. Visiting the homes of my students and traveling extensively in the Middle East, I learned another way of life. The eroded hills and small villages along rutted dirt roads, contrasting with ruins of ancient gymnasiums, large amphitheaters, and paved marble avenues, made a deep impression upon me, so I returned to Yale to study the conservation of natural resources. While earning my M.S. degree, I realized I was interested more in how people developed attitudes toward their physical environment than in specific techniques of land utilization. This led me to the discovery of a people who, while their neighbors had "mined the land" or "worn out several farms," maintained excellent productivity from ordinary acres. These people were the Old Order Amish, who formed the basis for my Ph.D. dissertation.

—Gertrude Enders Huntington

The Editors

The following is an account of how we set about designing the research and obtaining the data for the case study, *The Hutterites in North America.* Use of the personal pronoun refers to the senior author except for the section on "Living with the Colony People," which is written by Gertrude Huntington.

Author Trudy Huntington is flanked by two Hutterite girls, Trudy and Abigail, who were named after Trudy and her daughter.

ESTABLISHING CONTACT

The anthropologist who is aware of his own uniqueness, his peculiar training, language skills, background, and niche will utilize his experience and personal resources. There are certain peculiarities and circumstances that made it natural for me to study the Hutterites. I could speak conversational German and Pennsylvania German, for I was reared in the Amish culture. I had studied the Old Order Amish (Hostetler 1993), and I was familiar with the history, traditions, and literature of the Amish and Hutterites. Soon after my family was situated in a small faculty apartment in Edmonton, we were visited by five strong, bearded men. They were Hutterite elders who had come to the provincial capital on important legislative business. They explained that the law (Hostetler 1974) which had restricted them from buying land in Alberta was to be changed, possibly to be made more stringent for Hutterites. Having heard that a professor from Pennsylvania had moved into their province, they had sought me out, for they hoped that I could find a German language printer for them. This initial contact by the Hutterite leaders was mutually fortunate. I had not sought contact with them, but they had come to see me, which was important in maintaining the rapport that was to follow.

At that time I was teaching a class in minority groups, so I took my students to the capitol building to observe the legislative hearing. We found not five Hutterite elders, but twenty-six bearded elders seated before the Alberta legislature. Hostile statements were exchanged on the floor of the meeting, and those who opposed the Hutterites wanted to see them "put in their place." During the week of hearings, I met many other Hutterite elders. Intuitively, I realized the elders were accepting me as one of them. This acceptance was balanced by obligations to be their host and chauffeur in a strange city. I answered their questions about my background and about the Old Order Amish in the United States. I indulged in late-night discussions and exposed myself to constant sub-zero weather. The result was my coming down with pneumonia. The risks in this fieldwork did not involve poisonous snakes or amoebic dysentery but normal, unromantic hazards. Following my recovery, I visited as many colonies as I could. In a short time, my identity was established with virtually all colonies.

A PERIOD OF EVALUATION AND INCUBATION

Before beginning work on a major research project, I spent two years assessing the various possibilities for research. I made exploratory contacts with not only different Hutterite colonies, but also with government agencies, real estate agents, lawyers, salesmen, and neighbors of the Hutterites. I kept asking myself what in the Hutterite culture was significant for social science or instructive for the modern world. With a small grant from the university, I made limited investigations of population change, migration, and mortality patterns. From this exploratory work it became clear that here was an opportunity for basic research. The confidence placed in me by the colony leaders assured me of almost unlimited access to data of all types. Getting to the colonies for fieldwork was no major problem, for the colonies were within easy driving distance. Short trips were possible over weekends during the academic year and over longer periods during the holiday seasons. All of these factors were necessary considerations in thinking about what and how to undertake a research project that would have value.

The literature on the Hutterites was abundant, although most was in German. The printed materials pertaining to their history and religion had been published with the aid of sympathetic outsiders, such as university professors who already in the nineteenth century had gathered much of this material. The two large chronicles that the group had preserved had become the object of study by historians and philologists (Wolkan 1923; Zieglschmid 1947). Much of the material relevant to a cultural analysis was in manuscript form, written in Gothic script by the Hutterites themselves and handed down from generation to generation. Persons who could gain the confidence of the people and read the German material would have ready access to the data.

DELINEATING THE RESEARCH PROBLEM

Nonanthropological approaches to the study of Hutterites had to be distinguished from the anthropological approach in defining the research problem. What we wanted was a total picture of the culture so that insights could be secured that would apply inside or outside of the Hutterite culture. We were not interested in a manipulative study. We found interest, for example, among government agencies in a study of "the Hutterite problem," as it was called, but not from the perspective of basic social science research. Farm organizations passed amendments and resolutions at their annual meetings asking the government to do something about "the Hutterite problem." There were repeated references in area newspapers to "the Hutterite problem," with emotionally loaded phrases such as "spreading across Canada like locusts," "threaten the social and economic fibre of Alberta," "parasites," and "amoeba-like growth." "The Hutterite Investigation Committee" (Province of Alberta, 1959) had issued a report with recommendations soon after I arrived in Alberta. I attempted to interest these groups in a well-designed, long-range research project, but in this I failed. There was little support on the part of the provincial government or its agencies for research that promised no solutions to immediate problems. I then turned to sources in the United States and found support in the United States Office of Education, which provided funds for the study of socialization in various cultures.

After surveying the literature, assessing the availability of data, the probable cooperation of the colonies, and an adequate source of funds, the most promising research problem appeared to be a study of socialization. There were no systematic studies of Hutterite child-rearing practices, and in fact no anthropological analysis of the culture as a whole. It was clear that the group had achieved a remarkable record of survival through periods of internal disruption and external pressure. Hutterites were reputed to have great success in training their young to live communally. Few persons deserted colony life. Previous publications provided clues that led me to believe that an investigation of communal socialization patterns would be a basic contribution to knowledge. A few such clues are given below. In the seventeenth century a novelist said of the colonists: "There was no anger, no jealousy, no vengeful spirit, no envy, no concern about temporal things, no pride, no gambling, no remorse," and there was "altogether a lovely harmony" (Grimmelshausen 1668 in Friedmann 1956:583). A Russian government official who visited the colonies in 1818 reported that after the birth of a child, the mothers are assigned to separate quarters and are separated from their spouses a year-and-a-half (Zieglschmid 1947:420). The first sociologist who did fieldwork among the colonies stated that "the educational methods used by the Hutterites are training of the emotions rather than the intellect" and that "within each community a battle is being waged on an educational front between two widely different social orders, their own and ours" (Deets 1939:39, 45). Eaton and Weil (1955:41) reported unusual stability of the population and a low rate of desertion. Kaplan and Plaut (1956:104) concluded that the motivations that are built into the individual during socialization insure that the Hutterite "will want to do what he has to do."

THE RESEARCH DESIGN

The central purpose as stated in the research design was to acquire a knowledge of the methods of socialization (and indoctrination) in a highly collectivistically oriented society. Answers were sought to two fundamental questions: (1) Under what conditions and by what methods are moral values transmitted to children in a communal society?; (2) Under what conditions does the person who is trained for communal living deviate from the moral teachings of his society? In short, we wanted to know how individuals were equipped to live in a communal society, under what conditions individuals deviated from the norms of the society, and if they deserted the community, what adjustments were necessary to go from a communal society to one that was individualistic, as in modern industrialized society.

The research design incorporated what we believed to be the most relevant aspects of the culture: the formulation of the value orientation, the socialization activity in the community, and deviancy patterns. Within these areas of penetration we spelled out the different phases of the investigation—the problem, the method, personnel, and the budget.

The value orientation

We wanted an explicit account of the moral postulates of Hutterite culture. What was needed was the "charter" of the society that Malinowski (1944: 140, 162) called "the traditionally established values, programs, and principles of organized (institutional) behavior," or "the recognized purpose of the group." To understand socialization we wanted to know the goals individuals were trained to accept and to live by. We wanted to know the traditional charter (from their date of origins) and how contemporary Hutterites interpreted the meaning of the charter. We wanted to analyze the existing documents in the original language and to translate relevant sections into English.

The socialization patterns in the community

We wanted a knowledge of the environment within which learning takes place. We planned to make a field guide that would yield data on a wide range of subjects: maps of roads, buildings, entrances, and the like; topography, temperature, flora, and fauna; unusual environmental conditions such as hail, epidemics, droughts, pests; productivity of crops, livestock raising, and so forth. We wanted to distinguish between the "ideal" and "real" aspects of the community with respect to physical environment and to major social groupings, family and kinship patterns, leadership and authority, and patterns of interaction with outsiders. The field guide was prepared so that each subject had two parts: part A consisted of observed data by the fieldworker and part B consisted of the preferred pattern. For example, once we had a map of the roads and dwellings (observed data) we would ask the Hutterite informants what changes would be desirable, or "What would you do differently if you had to do it over again?" By this method we were able to compare the "observed" with the "preferred" patterns of culture and thereby acquire a knowledge of any gaps between "ideal" and "real" aspects of culture. Various guides for investigating socialization patterns from infancy to adulthood were planned. Formal and informal learning were to be observed. We wanted to ascertain the amount of exposure to non-Hutterite sources of knowledge, and to administer achievement tests where appropriate. Attention would be directed toward learning that was not specifically stated in the charter and to individuals who take seriously those beliefs that are not a part of the traditional values. To accomplish this work I wanted to have trained persons, ideally husband-wife teams, located in three colonies.

Deviancy patterns

In addition to observing deviancy patterns within the community, we planned to interview persons who had left the colonies, those who had left permanently as well as persons who had been away and returned. On the basis of previous studies, we believed that several dozen such persons could be found. We wanted to discover both the factors that attracted persons to the outside world and factors that repulsed persons from their Hutterite training and background. Depth interviews were planned (with an interview guide) to gather the necessary data. The data would reveal to what extent the deserters still evidenced the communally oriented morality, and what Hutterite attitudes toward property, religious values, and family relationships were maintained in the life of these persons after they were assimilated into the dominate culture.

ENTERING THE COMMUNITY

The first step after funds were approved for a research period of three-and-one-half years was to secure a panel of consultants and bring them to Edmonton for the initial overall planning. This panel was made up of persons representing various disciplines in the social sciences.[1] One of the consultants had participated in an earlier study of the mental health of the Hutterites. The panel gave valuable aid in improving the research design and in preparing the field guides. I met periodically with the panel during the operative period of the research to review the progress of the fieldwork.

In hiring fieldworkers I sought professionally trained persons rather than students, and married rather than single persons, preferably with competence in the German language. They had to be socially mature and in good health. Persons were needed who would be the least offensive to Hutterites and who would also be willing to reside in a Hutterite colony for several months at a time. My thought was that either the wife or the husband might teach in the colony school, while the other would devote major time in recording the observations. Fieldworkers would have to exercise great facility in accommodating to the Hutterite mode of living. Although I wanted persons who were sympathetic to Hutterite religion, I could not use persons who were inclined to be either too sympathetic or too argumentative. Since smoking is taboo, I could not hire fieldworkers who smoked. One of the reasons for choosing married persons is that among Hutterites, marriage is a mark of maturity and I wanted to make sure that we were admitted to the lifestyles of both male and female.

---

[1]The panel of consultants were Laura Thompson, anthropology; Calvin Redekop, sociology; Joseph H. Britton, family and child development; Bert Kaplan, psychology; Dale B. Harris, psychological testing; and Robert Friedmann, history.

A male fieldworker, for example, is decidedly limited in observing the life style of women in the colony.

The three colonies we chose for intensive observation were selected on the basis of their affiliation, geographic area, size, age, and willingness to cooperate. The objective was to observe the basic unit, which was a relatively small number of persons. The largest of the three sample colonies had eighteen married pairs and the smallest had eight. The combined population in the three colonies was 280 persons. We preferred maximum geographic and social distance between the communities so that there would be virtually no interaction among the colonies we observed. The colonies were located respectively in Manitoba, Alberta, and Montana. It was important that the colonies be "normal" rather than atypical. The Hutterite leaders gave courteous advice to us in this respect.

Contact with the Hutterites was maintained on several levels at the same time. There was the level of the principal investigator who secured the needed cooperation and maintained contact with the leadership, the fieldworkers who established a residence and a living relationship with the colonies, and persons who went in and out of the colonies obtaining specific data such as interviewing certain individuals. The fieldworkers who interviewed ex-Hutterites were not the same persons who established residence in the colonies. Each of us, it turned out, established rapport with different persons. Hutterite inclinations for making friends with outsiders varied greatly. The differences in the quality of the relationships established between investigators and informants varied with their personalities and roles. Each fieldworker became aware of those persons in the colony with whom he could establish least rapport. The principal investigator was usually engulfed by the preachers so that he often had limited freedom to talk with the younger people or to move about from one social category to another.

Before placing the professionally trained persons in the colonies, we assigned one fieldworker to visit all three colonies to secure certain kinds of records and information. Her task was to obtain a complete colony census, births, deaths, number of persons in various social categories, copies of school instructional materials, and the like. She remained one month in each of the three colonies, and the data obtained was then shared with the professionally trained fieldworkers prior to their taking up residence in the colony. Although this fieldworker was neither married nor trained professionally, she had all the needed qualifications to establish instantaneous friendships with Hutterite women. She was German-speaking, middle-aged, heavy rather than slender, had been in Europe over a span of several years in resettlement work, was adept at following copious instructions, and was willing to brave sub-zero weather with her Volkswagen. Her genuine friendliness and short stay in each of the colonies did much to establish an attitude of cooperation.

The principal fieldwork was done by Gertrude Huntington, who was trained as an anthropologist and who has had experience in relating to ethnic minorities. Of special significance was the involvement of her whole family in the fieldwork: her husband, David, who was a participant for the last part of the summer; their three children, Caleb, aged two-and-one-half, Daniel, aged five, and Abigail, aged nine; and her mother, Abbie Enders, who was a child psychologist and kindergarten teacher in Swarthmore, Pennsylvania, for many years. They established residence in the Alberta colony in the little house used by the teacher during the school year. The resident fieldworkers in the two other colonies were male school teachers, their wives, and children. The following section, "Living with the Colony People," is told by Gertrude Huntington.

LIVING WITH THE COLONY PEOPLE

Before my initial trip to the community, I met with other members of the research team, read available material on the Hutterites, obtained detailed data on the geology, climate, and soil—the physical properties of the immediate region, and familiarized myself with the names, ages, and relationships of the members of the colony. To be a full adult by Hutterite standards, a person must be married and have children. However, even when this status has been achieved, a woman is never completely adult in that she is not really independent. Even though she has children, she is always to be under the guidance of her husband, or if she is not with him, she is usually visiting her mother, who then supervises her. Therefore, I arranged it so that I was always with my mother or my husband, as well as with our three children during the period of participant observation. Only as a visitor did I go to a colony alone. I attempted to fill the role of a typical Hutterite woman of my age—a woman whose husband held no outstanding comminity position and a woman who did not have a special leadership role assigned to her. My mother, as the oldest woman in the community, was called "grandmother" by everyone and did only the work expected of older women. If she did not do some task because she was caring for our children or doing something related to the study, nothing was said, for women over fifty have this prerogative. However, I had to do all the expected colony work or I was sent for. Women of my age are excused only for illness or childbirth. Our three children were each of a different Hutterite age stage. The youngest, Caleb, was a "house child" and was treated as such by all the members of the community. We carried his food from the kitchen and fed him in the house, as was done for all the house children. Daniel was a "kindergartener." However, he was sent to the kindergarten only when my mother went too, to help or observe. The kindergarten was run on alternate days by the second and third oldest women in the community, so it was natural for my mother to visit. Abigail was nine and was, therefore, a "school child." She participated fully in the program for the school children, remaining under the direction of the German teacher for virtually all her waking hours. She ate her meals with the school children and did the community work required of them. The only part of the program she did not participate fully in was the memorizing of the long German verses and answering questions on the Sunday sermon. She attended all the meetings of the school children, all the religious services, and worked mornings for one of the families who did not have a girl old enough to clean and wax the floors. Because of our family structure, we were able to participate in every age level within the colony, except that of the adolescents. We were able to establish rapport with the adolescents, both because we were not part of the adult hierarchy and because we were sympathetic and discrete. Our daughter, Abigail, was sometimes admitted to the fringes of adolescent activities. When my husband joined us later in the summer, he participated in the general (in contrast to specialized or administrative) colony work of the adult men. Due to the structure of Hutterite society, our roles were determined by our age, sex, and marital status. Our task was to carry them out properly by Hutterite standards.

Our integration into the community was achieved in a series of steps. The first two days we were guests and visitors. The Hutterite children made a great fuss over our children and were very attentive and kind to them. During this brief period, we learned the physical layout of the central portion of the colony: the location of the longhouses and small houses in which the different families lived, the school house that also served as the church, the kitchen complex that contained the dining room, the laundry, bath house, and the pump house from which we carried our water. We ate all our meals in the communal dining hall, sitting in our assigned seats that were determined by our age, sex, and family relationship. The adults ate at one sitting, the school children at another, the kindergarteners ate in the kindergarten house or at home with the house children. We never ate as a family unit. We did our laundry at the assigned day and hour in the communal laundry and bathed at the accustomed time, waiting our turn at the community bathtub. We attended church each day with the adults and the school children, sitting in our assigned places.

As soon as it became evident that we were really trying to participate in the colony life rather than merely visiting or working on the fringes, we were urged to put away our "ugly" clothes and dress in correct Hutterite costume. Some of the women brought us used clothes that did not fit their children or that they were not wearing. Some was given to us, some was lent to us. Several of the better seamstresses offered to make us clothes for church and for Sunday if we would buy the material and the thread.

Among the Hutterites one's dress is extremely important as an emblem of classification. First, it signifies that one is a Hutterite; secondly, it proclaims the wearer's sex; thirdly, it indicates the type of activity the wearer will be engaged in; and finally, for women it signifies her acceptance of her position as subservient to men. The details of the costume also proclaim to the practiced eye the docility of the wearer in accepting the rules of his colony. In order to participate as Hutterites, we had to learn the details of grooming that would enable any Hutterite to classify us correctly.

Once we were really accepted, as signified by our dressing Hutterite, we felt all the pressures of the colony to conform. The degree of conformity required is difficult for an American to appreciate, for it affects virtually every detail of one's daily life, all one's actions, and almost every expression of one's thinking. Any evidence of individuality on our part was immediately resisted. When my mother found many of the small regulations, especially those pertaining to the lower status of women, irksome, the fellow colonists would imply that perhaps she was forgetful of them because she was so old. This was an effective means of soliciting conformity from one who is professionally competent as a school teacher and a child psychologist. With me, they would imply that the colony work was perhaps too demanding. As status is closely tied to one's ability to work hard, long, and fast, I tended to shape up and conform. Two of our three children were completely responsive to colony pressures and learned very quickly what was acceptable behavior.

After only a few days our two-and-one-half-year-old was observed to hit another toddler and then lean over and kiss him. Caleb already had learned that if you immediately kiss the child you hit, punishment is avoided at the hands of the baby sitters or adults. The first Hutterite word he learned was "kiss." He played happily with the other house children and enjoyed the solicitous attention of the adults. By the end of the summer he never spoke above a whisper in the presence of non-family adults. Our school child, Abigail, quickly internalized the rules of dress and conduct and corrected us privately if we deviated in the slightest degree from the excepted pattern. "Grandmother, that *vanic* (overblouse) is not right to wear on Saturday afternoon." "Mother, yesterday you laughed when you were talking to Leonard and Fred (adult Hutterite men)." She learned to act shy in the presence of adults and to show no other emotion unless she was alone with the children, joining in their rough and boisterous games.

The only member of our family who did not respond to social pressure was Daniel, our five-year-old boy, who was protected from full colony participation by keeping him out of the kindergarten and discouraging other adults from administering physical punishment. This is the age when "the stubborn will is broken" and by modifying the impact of the culture upon him, he was able to maintain a degree of

Abigail Huntington playing with a Hutterite school girl.

independence. This remained something of a problem throughout the period of participant observation, but it also enabled us to learn more about methods of child-training and peer-group pressure. Public opinion affected Daniel little, and the harsher his peers the harder he fought back. He responded to teasing with anger, which is not tolerated in Hutterite children, and on several occasions he yelled, which is also not sanctioned. The first Hutterite words he learned were expletive words, calling another child a dog or a pig, prefaced with a suitable adjective. His closest colony friend was boy two years older than he who was also somewhat excluded by the children and who probably profited by Daniel's presence as a target for the other children's teasing and hostility.

Participant observation required complete acceptance of the colony time schedule. The day is broken up into small units, with a constant change of activity. The speed with which a job is started and completed is stressed. Thus, dinner for the colony adults is eaten in seven to ten minutes, the dining room and kitchen are cleaned and the dishes for the dinner washed and put away in another seven minutes. One's activity is scheduled from the rising bell in the morning (at about 6:15) until after supper (about 7:00, unless there is extra work like haying or harvesting, or ducks to pluck).

At first, my mother, I, and even my husband had difficulty finishing our meal in the allotted time, and our school-age child often ate some of her brothers' food at home for she had not learned to eat fast enough to satisfy her hunger in the allotted time. The food was delicious, primarily of Russian peasant origin, with some unusual dishes. The heads were considered a choice part of the meat. Only the men were served the steer heads, but the women and the children were given duck heads, which we split and ate.

Families slept in their own apartment. We had a tiny house with two double beds for the five of us. At first we shared an outhouse with another family, but later they built one for us. There were no locks on the apartment doors and it was not the custom to knock before entering. We had a constant stream of people in and out from before breakfast in the morning until about 11:00 at night. Whether or not we were in the house made little difference, for colony members are free to go around as they wish. However, there are personal friendships and not everyone visits everyone else and some do not enter another's apartment if no family member is at home. We had a little trouble adjusting to the complete lack of privacy, but the preacher explained to us: "You are fortunate to be living in the colony, for here there are always one hundred eyes watching you." He went on to point out that this protected us from any chance deviation from the accepted pattern of behavior. Later, when I visited without my family, I was greeted as a relative and during the three days was never alone.

Personal needs could be indulged only within the system. Thus, we bought extra food and ate it or occasionally served it to fellow colonists late on a summer evening. Nice toilet soap to take to the community bath house instead of using the brown homemade soap for the Saturday afternoon bath became a type of personal luxury that was acceptable within the system. No one could leave the colony without the preacher's permission, and in this way too we conformed, for had we had freedom of movement we would have been too privileged. The only time during a seven-week stay that our family was outside the colony as a unit, our school-age child begged,

"Drive slowly, it is so easy to breathe out here." The detailed time schedule, the constant surveillance, and pressure to conform kept us always busy.

As participant observers we were careful not to be innovators. We attempted to support and adjust to the system as fully as we were able. Thus, I did not bring a radio or a camera with me (both forbidden possessions although widely used in secret by adolescents). We made an effort not to suggest alternative ways of doing things and not to introduce new activities or new ideas. Because a fairly large number of individuals were involved in the study, it was possible for different investigators to have completely different roles. The person who gathered the census data and specific information from interviews was never in the colony at the same time that we were and was not identified with our family. Photographs were obtained from other sources so that we would not betray their trust by breaking an important taboo. We attempted to be as inconspicuous as possible and largely succeeded, so that visitors to the colony never realized that we were not Hutterite. The only time I was recognized as non-Hutterite was after we had left our "home colony" and were on our way back to the States. Because we would be visiting other colonies on the way, we were still dressed Hutterite. I took our youngest child, who had bronchitis, to the doctor. During the examination I asked him about one of the ailing colony members and he answered using his best medical jargon. Without thinking, I responded with similar vocabulary. For the first time, he really looked at me and asked, "Who are you? You don't talk like a Hutterite woman."

On one occasion I stepped completely out of character as a submissive Hutterite woman, although even then I was careful to determine colony consensus before I acted. A lovely nineteen-year-old girl who was cooking for the colony became ill with boils. The one in the middle of her forehead swelled until her eyes shut and she had red streaks running towards her eye. She had a fever and was obviously very sick. This same day the three highest-ranking men in the colony, those who give permission to leave the colony for any reason, were away on business. The girl was becoming sicker in front of our eyes. Everyone visited her, clucked over her condition, and told her about people they knew who had died from boils. The feeling began to grow that she should be taken to the hospital, but the highest ranking man left in the colony was opposed. He did not believe in doctors. Everyone was critical of every possible course of action and no one was able to reach a decision or to do anything. Finally, with her mother's tacit permission, and the backing of the women, I took her to the nearest hospital. She was admitted immediately. By the time I returned, the leaders were back and everyone was relieved that the girl was safely in the hospital.

One can master the schedule of the day and the details of grooming more easily than the patterns of thought. I constantly came up against the fact that there was little cause and effect in the world. Newton, Descartes, and subsequent scientists have had minimal influence on the Hutterite world view. Everything happens according to God's plan. One day an adult Hutterite man who was in town was approached by a stranger who said, "I'm a religious man, but I don't belong to a church."

"That's too bad," said the Hutterite. "If you are a religious man you should support a church."

"No, no. I can't take that Virgin Mary stuff," replied the stranger.

"Do you believe that God created the universe?" asked the Hutterite.

"Of course, I believe that God created the world."

The Hutterite replied: "If God created the whole world, then one virgin birth shouldn't be too difficult."

Once their premises are accepted, the Hutterites have an answer or a proverb for every question.

In the northern plains, where this colony was located, there is a constant threat of hail. Three times the colony had suffered severe hail damage, and it was always a race to get the grain harvested in time. This had been a good growing season; the crop was heavy and ripe. The combines were ready, and finally they cut one trial swath around a single field. The decision was to begin combining the following day. But next morning we awakened to rain. My husband and I were distressed; the colonists had worked hard all summer, yet everyone seemed calm. The second day we woke to continued rain. We said to the preacher, "Aren't you worried? It's raining." He smiled gently and said, shrugging his shoulders, "What can you do?" The third day the rain continued; it was cold and damp. In contrast to the colonists, we were quite frantic. "It is still raining," we announced in rather critical tones. The minister turned to us and said severely, "You know Who makes it rain." On another occasion I had been the last woman to wash, and before my clothes were dry it began to rain. The woman closest to me in age, who had washed early, came to help me take them off the clothes line and bring them in. As I hurriedly snatched them down, I commented, "I don't see why it has to rain every Monday." "To teach us patience," she quietly answered. The major problem I had was not in adjusting to any of the details of life or work, different or difficult as they might be, but to base my actions on the concept, so central to Hutterite colony life, of *Gelassenheit,* or full resignation. It is very difficult for someone raised in our individualistic American culture to think and act as a passive instrument, to renounce all self-will, exchanging it for patience and self-surrender to the colony. Yet, this is necessary if the participant is to experience the joys as well as the tribulations of colony life and if he is to understand the deep satisfaction of the Hutterite way of life.

Full participation in a Hutterite colony demands about eighteen hours a day, seven days a week, so there was very little time for writing while in the field. I kept a series of 8-inch by 5-inch spiral notebooks: one journal on food, recipes, and home remedies, one on women's work and activities, one on men's work and activities (kept largely by my husband), one on movement to and from the colony, and three miscellaneous notebooks. Every moment of privacy I used to talk into a tape-recorder, which was always set up, except that I kept the tape hidden so that it could not be listened to in my absence. As soon as a tape was filled, it was mailed off. My mother, husband, and the children also recounted incidents into the tape-recorder. This material averaged about fifty typed pages a week. There was always the feeling that had there been more hours in the day more material could have been recorded more fully.

There is not room in a Hutterite colony for a long-term visitor, and Hutterites dislike prying questions even when asked by fellow members. Their contacts with "outsiders" are stylized and frequently superficial. Therefore, if one is to study such things as the total culture—lifestyles, child-rearing, the role of women—one must really participate. Only on the physical, working-living level can real relationships be built and meanings and feelings that are never verbalized, be observed. The anthropologist needs to know enough about the culture in advance and be sensitive when he first arrives, if he is to find an acceptable role. The great advantage to be gained from having a whole family enter a community must be weighed against the demands the researcher's family makes on him and the effect of a number of people entering the community. Children are excellent observers and reporters, but one must consider both the long- and short-term effect of the experience on one's own children. In his interest and excitement to learn about culture, the anthropologist must remember that individuals are more than cultural representations or sources of information. In the final analysis, we are working with the real lives of real people and we must not "use" either our own families or members of the host culture primarily as "tools" to further an abstraction. The individuals, the society, or the culture should not be destroyed or painfully injured by our study.

CONCLUDING OBSERVATIONS

We have discussed some of the special problems encountered in doing fieldwork among the Hutterites. It is not suggested that our work among the Hutterites is representative of the kind of problems the anthropologist would encounter in other ethnic groups. Some of the methods we have used can be applied to the study of other cultures, but the details of relating anthropologically to each culture will vary. Effective fieldwork involves not only learning all one can from the discipline, but also adapting one's personal resources, uniquenesses, and individual experiences. We will conclude with some general observations on fieldwork, terminating the research, interpreting the findings, and maintaining contacts with the society.

The role of the participant observer and the nonparticipating observer differ greatly. The nonparticipating observer comes in contact with the culture for a limited time, usually to obtain information on a specific aspect of the group: its economic and agricultural practices, its origins, old books and manuscripts, or perhaps to obtain blood samples. The anthropologist who is interested in the total culture will become a participant in the work and inner life of the community. Participation is possible insofar as the individual is acceptable to the group. Hutterites, like the Old Order Amish and other ethnic groups, are very quickly able to judge the motives and sincerity of the prospective participant. Once the participant observer has accepted the roles and the work responsibility of the colony, he is obligated to help support the traditions and the taboos of his age set. The nonparticipating observer can often flout the taboos because he is presumed ignorant of the colony standards. The colony can only accommodate him for a brief period, for an extended stay would introduce disruptive elements into the culture. Since Hutterites are willing to accept converts, they are perhaps less suspicious and more receptive to outsiders than some ethnic groups. Some individuals tried to persuade us to join the colony, and some generously offered to assist us in organizing a "colony" in our home communities. The degree of openness to outsiders varied greatly among colonies.

The time spent in analyzing the findings and preparing the research report was more than three times that spent doing fieldwork. After the research report was completed, we proceeded to outline and write the case study. Return trips to the colonies were advantageous. Observing a colony when it is newly founded and again at later stages when its population and its prosperity have increased yielded still additional insights.

Termination of the fieldwork presented no major problems. Many personal relationships had been formed during the course of fieldwork, which now had to be physically terminated but not altogether severed, for return visits were anticipated and communication by letter is possible. We were careful not to make others dependent upon us, but also to reward the colony in ways that were approved by the culture. Many exchanges were reciprocal. We typed colony letters or documents and occasionally obtained old or rare German books they wanted. The colony was especially inclined to give us gifts of produce, chicken, duck, bread, vegetables, braided rugs, pillows, and also small articles they had bought in stores.

Our fieldwork is formally terminated, but our relationships and ties with the Hutterites will never terminate. As participants we gained their friendships and invested a great deal of ourselves. They are a part of our lives. Just as they are always ready to take back their few stray members who have left the colonies, so also they are ready to take us back. On leaving the colony we were told, "When you come back we will greet you as a relative."

POSTSCRIPT

During the thirty years since this narrative was first written, we have returned many times. Children have grown up, married, and had children of their own. Friends have died. Daughter colonies have been successfully established. And our relationships and ties with our Hutterite friends continue to enrich our lives.

Appendix B / Table Rules

The following "Table Rules" are memorized by the *Darius-Leut* school children and recited daily before going to the dining hall. The use of such manners or guidelines was widespread in European countries among both German- and English-speaking people. Their purpose was to teach the first principles of family life and government in a well-ordered society. Not only Hutterites but also Puritan and Shaker communities taught their children manners at home, church, and table.

In table prayer be serious
And fold your hands in love,
Always in reverence lifting up
Your heart to God above

And when the prayer is ended
Turn left and right expressing
To neighbors each your wish that God
Upon this meal grant blessing.

You must never seat yourself
Ahead of all others
Because that is the surest mark
Of most ill-mannered brothers

Then do not upset your chair
Before you hold it fast,
And do not turn the serving dish
The way you like it best.

You must never be the first
To reach for food; no, wait
With patience till the older ones
First have filled their plates.

Do not always grasp
For only the best pieces
Or people will soon think
That with you all modesty ceases.

If a food is not prepared
The way you most would have it,
Do not speak up at once and say,
"I won't eat any of it."

You must not ask questions
About the food that's offered you,
And to not put your nose upon
The dishes passed before you.

Don't crunch things with your teeth
Or people will have fear
That wild beasts in the neighborhood
Are coming very near.

Don't dip into the salt dish
Your little bit of food,
Nor put your fingers in it,
For that is very rude.

Keep your elbows off the table
When you eat your food,
Otherwise your tablemates
Will think you very crude.

Hold your feet still while you're sitting
And keep your back up straight,
For a great amount of wiggling
Might damage cup and plate

Handle glasses carefully
Especially when they're filled,
For if they're held up shakily
Something might be spilled.

Do not disturb your tablemates
With irritation great
By licking each crumb greedily
From your empty plate.

If you have to blow your nose
You must do it right;
Do not let it trumpet forth
And fill everyone with fright.

But turn politely to the side
To give yourself relief.
Wipe your nose with skill and speed
Using your handkerchief.

When yawning quickly raise your hand
To hide your mouth from view,
So that your neighbor need not fear
You will devour him, too.

If you get the urge to sneeze
Meet it with good grace;
Promptly hold your handkerchief
Up before your face.

When the meal comes to an end
Be thankful for the food.
Be ready with great happiness
To pray in gratitude.

For God has called each one of us
His loving child to be,
That we may in our faith persist
To serve him joyfully.

Amen.

Source: Gesang-Buchlein: Lieder für Schule und häuslichen Gebrauch
(Cayley, Alberta, Canada: 1961, p. 86). Tr. by Elizabeth Bender and Ilse Reist.

Bibliography

Alberta, Province of, 1949, *Report of the Hutterite Investigation Committee.* Edmonton, Alberta, Canada. September 1959.

American Journal of Medical Genetics, 1985, Special issue on genetic diseases among Hutterite populations. November, Vol. 22, No. 3.

Arnold, Eberhard, 1964, *Eberhard Arnold, A Testimony of Church-Community from his Life and Writings.* Rifton, New York: Plough Publishing House.

Bennett, John W., 1967, *The Hutterian Brethren: Agriculture and Social Organization in a Communal Society.* Stanford, Calif.: Stanford University Press.

Bolt, Edward D. and Roberts, Lance W., 1980, "The Decline of Hutterite Population Growth: Causes and Consequences — a Comment," *Canadian Ethnic Studies,* XII, No. 3, pp. 111–117.

Bolken-Zumpe, Elizabeth, 1994, *Torches Extinguished: Memories of a Communal Bruderhof Childhood in Paraguay, Europe and the USA.* San Francisco, California: The Pereguine Foundation.

Canadian Mental Health Association, 1953, *The Hutterites and Saskatchewan: A Study of Inter-group Relations.* Regina, Saskatchewan.

Clark, Bertha W., 1924, "The Hutterian Communities," *Journal of Political Economy,* Vol. 32, pp. 357–374 and 468–486.

Conkin, Paul K., 1964, *Two Paths to Utopia: The Hutterites and the Llano Colony.* Lincoln, Neb.: The University of Nebraska Press.

Constitution of the Hutterian Brethren Church and Rules as to Community of Property, 1950; 1993.

Deets, Lee Emerson, 1939, *The Hutterites: Study in Social Cohesion.* Gettysburg, Pa.: Times and News Publishing Co. Ph.D. dissertation, Faculty of Political Science, Columbia University.

Durnbaugh, Donald F., 1991, "Relocation of the German Bruderhof to England, South America, and North America," *Communal Studies,* 62–77.

Eaton, Joseph W., 1952, "Controlled Acculturation," *American Sociological Review,* June, pp. 331–340.

Eaton, Joseph W., 1958, "Folk Obstetrics and Pediatrics Meet the M.D.: A Case Study of Social Anthropology and Medicine," *Patients, Physicians, and Illness,* edited by E. Gartley Jaco. Glencoe, Ill.: Free Press.

Eaton, Joseph W., 1964, "The Art of Aging and Dying," *Gerontologist,* Vol. 4, No. 2, pp. 94–101.

Eaton, Joseph W., and Albert J. Mayer, 1954, *Man's Capacity to Reproduce: The Demography of a Unique Population.* New York: Free Press. Reprinted from *Human Biology,* Vol. 25, No. 3.

Eaton, Joseph W., and Robert Weil, 1955, *Culture and Mental Disorders: A Comparative Study of Hutterites and Other Populations.* Glencoe, Ill.: Free Press.

Eliade, Mircea, 1961, *The Sacred and the Profane.* New York: Harper & Row, Harper Torchbook edition.

Flint, David, 1975, *The Hutterites. A Study in Prejudice.* Toronto: Oxford University Press.

Friedmann, Robert, 1956, "Grimmelshausen, Hans Jakob" s.v. *Mennonite Encyclopedia*, v. II, 583–584.

Friedmann, Robert, 1961, *Hutterite Studies*. Goshen, Ind.: Mennonite Historical Society.

Friedmann, Robert, 1965, *Die Schriften der Huterischen Täufergemeinschaften. Gesamtkalog Ihrer Manuskriptbücher. Ihrer Schreiver und Ihrer Literatur 1529–1667*. Wein: Hermann Böhlaus Nachf.

Gesang-Büchlein: Lieder für Schule und Hauslichen Gebrauch (Cayley, Alberta, Canada: 1961, p. 86–89). Tr. by Elizabeth Bender and Ilse Reist.

Gross, Leonard, 1980, *The Golden Years of the Hutterites 1565–1578*. Scottdale, Pa.: Herald Press.

Gross, Paul A., 1965, *The Hutterite Way*. Saskatoon, Saskatchewan: Freeman Publishing Company.

Hoebel, E. Adamson, 1966, *Anthropology: The Study of Man*, 3rd ed. New York: McGraw-Hill.

Hofer, Peter, 1955, *The Hutterian Brethren and Their Beliefs*. Starbuck, Manitoba: The Hutterian Brethren of Manitoba. Approved by the Committee of Elders.

Hofer, Joshua, 1985, *Japanese Hutterites: A Visit to Owa Colony*, rev. ed. Elie, Manitoba: James Valley Book Center.

Hofer, John, 1988, *The History of the Hutterites*. Elie, Manitoba: Educational Committee, James Valley Colony.

Holzach, Michael, 1993, *The Forgotten People: A Year Among the Hutterites*. Sioux Falls, South Dakota.

Horsch, John, 1931, *The Hutterite Brethren 1528–1931: A Story of Martyrdom and Loyalty*. Goshen, Ind.: Mennonite Historical Society.

Hostetler, John A., 1974, *Hutterite Society*. Baltimore: Johns Hopkins University Press.

Hostetler, John A., 1993, *Amish Society*, 4th ed. Baltimore: Johns Hopkins Press.

Huntington, Gertrude, 1981, "Children of the Hutterites," *Natural History* 90, 2:34–47.

Huntington, Gertrude E., 1987, "Order Rules the World: Our Children Among the Communal Society of the Hutterites." In *Children and Anthropological Research*, Barbara Butler and Diane Turner, eds. New York: Plenum Press, 53–71.

Hutterian Brethren, trans. and ed., 1987. *The Chronicle of Hutterian Brethren, Volume I*. Plough Publishing House, Rifton, New York.

Hutterian Brethren, Trans. ed. 1988. *Brothers Unite: An Account of the Uniting of Eberhard Arnold and the Röhn Bruderhof with the Hutterian Church*. Plough Publishing House, Ulster Park, New York.

Hutterian Brethren Church, 1950, "Constitution of the Hutterian Brethren Church and Rules as to Community of Property." Winnipeg, Manitoba: E. A. Fletcher, Barrister-Solicitor. Rev. 1993.

Hutterischen Brüder, 1962, *Die Lieder der Hutterischen Brüder*. Cayley, Alberta.

Hutterischen Brüdern in Kanada, 1961, *Gesang-Büchlein. Lieder für Schule und hauslichen Gebrauch*. Cayley, Alberta.

Ingoldsby, Bron B., and Max E. Stanton, 1988, "The Hutterites and Fertility Control, " *Journal of Comparative Family Studies*, Vol. 19, No l. (Spring) 137–141.

Janzen, Rod A., 1986, *Terry Miller: The Pacifist Politician. From Hutterite Colony to State Capitol*. Freeman, S. Dak.: Pine Hill Press.

Jeschke, Marlin, 1993, "The Church Discipline Case Among the Hutterites of Manitoba." Paper, Communal Studies Association, October 14–17.

Kaplan, Bert, and Thomas F. A. Plaut, 1956, *Personality in a Communal Society*. Lawrence, Ks.: University of Kansas Publications.

Kluckhohn, Clyde, 1949, "The Philosophy of the Navaho Indians," in *Ideological Differences and World Order*, ed. F. S. C. Northrop, New Haven, Conn.: Yale University Press, 356–383.

KIT (Keep in Touch) Newsletter. A project of the Peregrine Foundation, P.O. Box 460141, San Francisco, CA 94146-0141.

Klaassen, Peter J., 1964, *The Economics of Anabaptism 1525–1560.* The Hague: Mouton and Co.

Kleinsasser, Samuel, 1994, "Our Broken Relationship with the Society of Brothers." Concord Colony, Manitoba.

Laing, L. M., 1980, "Declining Fertility in a Religious Isolate: The Hutterite Population of Alberta, Canada, 1951–1971," *Human Biology* (May) 52(2): 288–310.

Lang, Hartman, and Ruth Gohlen, 1985, "Completed Fertility of the Hutterites: A Revision," *Current Anthropology,* Vol. 26, No. 3:395.

Littell, Franklin H., 1958, *The Anabaptist View of the Church,* 2nd ed. Boston: Starr King Press.

Lorimer, Frank, et al., 1954, *Culture and Human Fertility.* Paris: UNESCO.

Mackie, Marlene, 1965, "The Defector from the Hutterite Colony." M.A. thesis, University of Alberta.

Malinowski, Bronislaw, 1944, *A Scientific Theory of Culture and Other Essays.* Chapel Hill: University of North Carolina Press.

Mange, Arthur P., 1964, "Growth and Inbreeding of a Human Isolate" *Human Biology* 36(2):(May) 104–133.

Myers, Isabel Briggs, 1993, *Introduction to Type,* 5th ed., rev. by Linda K. Kirby and Katharine D. Myers. Palo Alto, Calif.: Consulting Psychologists Press, Inc.

Nordhoff, Charles, 1961, *The Communistic Societies of the United States.* New York: Hillary House Publishers. Original ed., 1875.

Palmer, Howard, 1971, "The Hutterite Land Expansion Controversy in Alberta," *Western Journal of Canadian Anthropology,* II, No. 2 (July), 18–46.

Palmer, Howard, 1972, *Land of the Second Chance: A History of Ethnic Groups in Southern Alberta.* Lethbridge, Alberta: The Lethbridge Herald.

Peter, Karl A., 1987, *The Dynamics of Hutterite Society: An Analytical Approach.* Edmonton, Alberta: University of Alberta Press.

Peters, Victor, 1965, *All Things Common: The Hutterian Way of Life.* Minneapolis: University of Minnesota Press.

Pratt, William F., 1969, "The Anabaptist Explosion," *Natural History,* (February), 8–23.

Priestly, David T., 1959, *A Study of Selected Factors Related to Attitude Toward the Hutterites of South Dakota.* Master's thesis, South Dakota State College.

Rideman, Peter, 1950, *Account of Our Religion. Doctrine and Faith.* Bungay, Suffolk, England: Hodder and Stoughton, Ltd., in conjunction with the Plough Publishing House. Trans. by K. E. Hasenberg from the German edition of 1565.

Riley, Marvin P., and David T. Priestly, 1959, "Agriculture on South Dakota's Communal Farms," *South Dakota Farm and Home Research,* Vol. 10, No. 2, Agricultural Experiment Station, South Dakota State College.

Ryan, John, 1977, *The Agricultural Economy of Manitoba Hutterites.* Toronto: Carleton Library.

Sahlins, Marshall D. 1965, "On the Sociology of Primitive Exchange" in *The Relevance of Models for Social Anthropology* London: Tavistock.

Sanders, Douglas, 1964, "The Hutterites: A Case Study in Minority Rights," *Canadian Bar Review* (May), 225–242.

Schluterman, S., and E. Schluterman, 1969, "Social Role Perception of Children in Hutterite Society," *Journal of Psychology,* LXXII, 183–188.

Serl, Vernon C., 1964, *Stability and Change in Hutterite Society.* Ph.D. dissertation, University of Oregon.

Smith, C. Henry, 1981, *The Story of the Mennonites,* 5th ed. Newton, Ks.: Mennonite Publication Office.

Smucker, Donovan E., ed., 1977, *The Sociology of Canadian Mennonites. Hutterites and Amish: A Bibliography with Annotations,* Vols. I and II. Waterloo, Ontario, Canada.

Spiro, Melford, 1958, *Children of the Kibbutz.* Cambridge, Mass.: Harvard University Press.

Steele, C. Frank, 1941, "Canada's Hutterite Settlement," *Canadian Geographical Journal* (June). Vol. 22: 308–314.

Stephenson, Peter H., 1991, "The Hutterian People: Ritual and Rebirth Symbols in the Evolution of Communal Life." University Press of America.

Weber, Max, 1930, *The Protestant Ethic and the Spirit of Capitalism.* Trans. by Talcott Parsons. London: Allen and Unwin.

Whitworth, John M., 1975, *God's Blueprints: A Sociological Study of Three Utopian Sects,* pp. 167–219. London: Routledge and Kegan Paul.

Wilson, Bryan R., 1959, "An Analysis of Sect Development," *American Sociological Review,* Vol. 24, pp. 3–15.

Wolkan, Rudolf, 1923, *Geschicht-Buch der Hutterishen Brüder.* Vienna, Austria, and Standoff Colony, Alberta.

Zablocki, Benjamin, 1971, *The Joyful Community.* Baltimore, Md.: Penguin. 1980 second ed. Chicago: University of Chicago.

Zieglschmid, A. J. F., 1947, *Das Klein-Gesichtsbuch der Hutttischen Brüder.* Philadelphia: Carl Schurz Memorial Foundation.

INSTRUCTIONAL FILMS: VHS VIDEO CASSETTE

The Hutterites, produced by Canada's National Film Board in 1962, is a favorite of many classroom instructors. B&W, 28 minutes. It is available from Canada's Film Distribution Center, Feinberg Library, SUNY, Plattsburgh, NY 12901. Tel.: (518) 564-2396. FAX: (518) 564-5209.

A documentary film of contemporary Hutterites in color is entitled *The Hutterites: To Care and Not To Care.* It was produced by RHB Productions in 1991. 58 and 29 minutes. It is available from Gateway Films for rental or purchase: 2030 Wentz Church Road, Worcester, PA 19490. Tel.: (215) 584-1893. Fax: (215) 584-4610.

CREDITS AND ACKNOWLEDGMENTS

All photos taken by the authors unless otherwise noted.

The authors are indebted to the following for photographs and permission to re-produce them. Copyright for each belongs to the photographer, unless otherwise specified.

Cover photo by John L. Ruth

Page xii Photo by Mary Koga
Page xiii Photo by Mary Koga
Page 11 Photo by Kryn Taconis
Page 15 Photo by Philip Garvin
Page 22 Photo by Philip Garvin
Page 24 Illustration by Lee Hopple and Muriel Kirkpatrick
Page 28 Photo by Philip Garvin
Page 44 Photo by Philip Garvin
Page 45 Photo by Philip Garvin
Page 49 Photo by Larry Porteaus
Page 70 Photo by Duff Marshall in *The Swift Current Sun*
Page 74 Photo by Philip Garvin
Page 92 Photo by Mary Koga
Page 105 Photo by Gerald Wright in *The Steinbach Carillon*
Page 120 Photo by John L. Ruth
Page 126 Photo by Gerald Wright in *The Steinbach Carillon*

Index